DIRECTION AND MANAGEMENT OF CHILDREN'S INSTITUTIONS AND AGENCIES

DIRECTION AND MANAGEMENT OF CHILDREN'S INSTITUTIONS AND AGENCIES

Responsible Guidance and Procedures

By

ERWIN H. PLUMER, ACSW

Youth Services Associates
Durham, North Carolina

CHARLES C THOMAS • PUBLISHER
Springfield • Illinois • U.S.A.

Published and Distributed Throughout the World by
CHARLES C THOMAS • PUBLISHER
2600 South First Street
Springfield, Illinois 62794-9265

This book is protected by copyright. No part of
it may be reproduced in any manner without
written permission from the publisher.

© *1989 by* CHARLES C THOMAS • PUBLISHER
ISBN 0-398-05551-3
Library of Congress Catalog Card Number: 88-30073

With THOMAS BOOKS *careful attention is given to all details of manufacturing and design. It is the Publisher's desire to present books that are satisfactory as to their physical qualities and artistic possibilities and appropriate for their particular use.* THOMAS BOOKS *will be true to those laws of quality that assure a good name and good will.*

Printed in the United States of America
Q-R-3

Library of Congress Cataloging in Publication Data
Plumer, Erwin H.
    Direction and management of children's institutions and agencies: responsible guidance and procedures/by Erwin H. Plumer.
    p. cm.
Bibliography: p.
Includes index.
ISBN 0-398-05551-3
    1. Child welfare--United States--Management. 2. Trusts and trustees--United States. I. Title.
HV741.P54 1989
362.7'068--dc19   88-30073
                                                        CIP

FOREWORD

THIS BOOK is really about children, because institutions exist for the sake of children. Children are the disenfranchised in our society: they have no vote, no political clout, few to lobby for them. All of the more than one hundred thousand children who live in institutions are separated from their families, and they depend upon the good will and professional competence of total strangers to guarantee them not only safety, but recognition of their intrinsic worth, a reasonable chance to grow and mature, education in accordance with their abilities, acknowledgement of their individuality, and a chance to rejoin their families.

Today's institutional children are not orphans, they have families. Many of those families are intact, many are separated. Whatever brought the child to the institution in the first place was not the child's problem alone; it was a problem within the family system. The family is an indelible, indivisible part of the child; the child and the family cannot be considered or treated as unrelated to each other. The child and the family constitute the client system of the agency.

The real challenge of the social welfare system is to prevent family breakdown. A child and his family belong together, and services should be directed at keeping them together. Preventing family breakdown is not always possible, however: problems are too deep-seated, complex, or long-lasting; resources for problem remediation are too few, intervention comes too late. As a result, some children must be separated from their families, at least for a time, and some of these children are appropriately placed in institutional care.

Recent developments in child welfare have identified the unique strengths and weaknesses of institutional care; they have identified the children who are properly referred for such care. Institutions are not to be used as a placement of convenience or last resort, when no other placement can be found. When separation of a child from his family is considered, careful evaluation of the needs of the child and of his family indicate the type of alternate care which is appropriate. Only the children who need the unique strengths of institutions should be admitted to them.

The welfare system and children and their families depend upon institutions to provide the most appropriate, professional care available. Each institution must have its program clearly formulated and professionally staffed; it must have a clear idea of the kinds of problems it can best remediate; and it must have the integrity not to attempt to provide services beyond its capability. Failing this, parental neglect or abuse may simply be replaced by state neglect or abuse.

No institution that provides competent service need be apologetic about being an institution. Today and for the foreseeable future, there is and will be need for professional institutional care.

Children and their families depend upon the institution for professional, compassionate help. The institutions depend upon members of the Boards of Directors. Boards of Directors determine the fate of children and their families.

PREFACE

THE BOARD OF DIRECTORS of a children's agency is the key to the success or failure of a children's institution and the institution's program and, hence, to the health and well-being of children in care. Executive directors and other staff members may come and go, but the Board continues, and, simply by continuing, it provides continuity and stability to the agency through the years.

To the extent that the Board is cognizant of its responsibilities and fulfills them, the agency will likely prosper, and children and their families will find healing and nurture. In the absence of an adequate Board, at best the agency will function at the mercy of the administration; at worst it may replicate the conditions which brought the children to the institution in the first place. Institutional abuse, maltreatment, or neglect is even more reprehensible than family neglect, for the institution purports to offer something better. The price of an inadequate Board is an inadequate agency.

The Board of Directors has multiple responsibilities: it has a responsibility to the supporting constituents of the agency; it has a responsibility to the executive director and, through him, to the other staff members of the agency; it has a responsibility to the children in care and their families; and it has a responsibility to the professional field in which the agency operates.

For virtually all children's agencies, Board membership is a voluntary activity. Personal expenses of Board members are reimbursed, but no salary or honorarium is involved. Board membership is a time- and energy-consuming task; it is a responsibility not to be undertaken lightly, because it involves the lives of children and their families.

The agency program may spell the difference between a child's becoming a mature, self-respecting, self-disciplined, productive adult and his becoming a permanent welfare case. In crass terms, the program may turn out a taxpayer or tax consumer. The agency program will certainly be instrumental either in helping a child and his family to reunite or else to ensure that they will forever remain separated.

Boards of children's institutions do not generally have a particularly good record in directing the agency for which they are responsible, or for developing structure and procedures which enable them to perform their task efficiently and effectively. Across the child care field, boards have fallen into various traps, of which the following are examples:

- some Boards have become rubber stamps for the executive director, granting all of his requests without question;
- some Boards immerse themselves in details of agency operations, and in the process lose the long-range vision for the agency;
- some Boards serve as a social stepping stone—persons who wish to climb the social ladder in some communities use Board membership to build a social dossier to achieve goals of their own;
- some Boards allow themselves to be dominated by a few strong Board members who may have personal agendas which may or may not be consistent with the agency agenda;
- some Boards permit the executive committee to become the *defacto* Board, with the whole Board automatically, without discussion or question, permitting the executive committee to rule;
- some Boards fail to build into the agency system checks which will alert the Board to the fact that their policies are being subverted;
- some Boards fail to construct and maintain limits around the executive director which compel him to perform within Board expectations;
- some Boards select board members in a cavalier manner and, once selected, fail to orient them to the work of the agency and of the Board or to assign them to meaningful tasks.

A well-organized and efficient board is the central strength of a children's agency. The effective Board selects its members planfully, orients them thoroughly, and utilizes them fully in accordance with their special competence. The Board keeps on top of the present work and focuses its energies on future problems and potential of the agency. The Board employs a competent executive director to administer the Board's policies, gives him latitude within prescribed limits, and supports him fully. The Board ensures that a quality program is offered and is adequately funded.

Some Boards are efficient and effective, of course. The Board and the administration are well organized and offer coordinated, professional services to children and their families. They are to be commended. May their number increase! For such Boards, this book will serve most effectively as a checklist and reminder.

The book is designed especially to assist the Board which is struggling—or which ought to be struggling—to organize itself, its work, and its agency in a manner that will discharge the work of the Board efficiently and effectively, provide for proper administration, adequate funding, and a program of excellence for children and their families.

This book is also for the new Board member and for Board members who have not considered boardmanship in its totality, who have joined a Board in order to be useful, but are unclear as to what it (Board membership) really entails.

This is really a "how-to" book for Boards. It provides a rationale for Board organization and functioning, with specific suggestions. Additionally, Part II presents some basic principles and concepts of residential child care which every Board member should have.

If Board members are able to perceive the work of the agency and the nature of children and staff from a fresh, professional perspective, the book's purpose will have been served, for knowledgeable Boards and Board members will provide appropriate and competent service to children and their families who need help.

Board membership in a children's agency should be an exciting and rewarding volunteer activity. Understanding what Boards of Directors are all about will enhance the excitement and increase the rewards.

Note: The pronoun "he" is used throughout the book in its generic sense, to denote either male or female. It should go without saying that Board members, executive directors, staff members, and residents can appropriately be male or female. No discrimination or chauvinism is intended; it is just simpler that way.

CONTENTS

Page

Foreword v
Preface vii

Part I The Board of Directors

Chapter 1: Purpose and Responsibility of Boards 3
Chapter 2: Board Organization 21
Chapter 3: The Executive Director 31
Chapter 4: Board/Staff Relationships 39
Chapter 5: Committees 55
Chapter 6: The Board Meeting 85

Part II Principles and Concepts of Residential Child Care

Chapter 7: Supplemental Parenting 99
Chapter 8: Per Capita Cost and Occupancy Rate 107
Chapter 9: Continuum of Care 115
Chapter 10: Permanency Planning 121

Bibliography 125
Index 127

DIRECTION AND MANAGEMENT
OF
CHILDREN'S INSTITUTIONS AND AGENCIES

Part I THE BOARD OF DIRECTORS

Chapter 1

PURPOSE AND RESPONSIBILITY OF BOARDS

The basic responsibility of a Board of Directors is to do the following:
- represent the supporting constituency
- specify an agency mission
- make long-range plans for the agency
- provide the budget to fund the program
- ensure appropriate use of agency assets
- provide accountability of funds and property entrusted to or acquired by the agency
- provide policies within which the program will be conducted to fulfill the mission
- provide an administrative structure to implement the agency program
- hire an executive director
- ensure that a program of professional excellence is operated for children in care

The Board of Directors must accommodate many factors:
- Each Board contains its own politics
- An agency which is sponsored by a larger organization such as a religious denomination or fraternal order must work within the politics of that organization and may have to compete for funds with other agencies or institutions sponsored by the same organization

- Most charitable organizations have had a financial struggle in recent years, in view of decreased state and federal funds and in view of the professional emphasis on deinstitutionalization
- Diminished numbers of children are being referred for institutional care, which means that the institutional beds may not be full.

Additionally, administrative theory says that institutions tend to take on a life of their own; after a few years the purpose of the institution may be quite different from the purpose for which it was founded.

Supporters tend to think of institutions as they existed a generation ago, caring for enchanting and well-behaved children who simply need a place to live; supporters feel good about vicariously providing service to children, and they assume that the institution is doing all that it should be doing in the way it should be doing it. Once entrenched in the hierarchy of a sponsoring organization or of a community, the institution receives memorials, bequests, and gifts of various kinds; it is included in the wills of interested citizens to the extent that closing the institution would be an embarrassment and require more explanations than most Boards are prepared to give.

Because of such reasons, the primary focus of the Board may come to be institutional survival, and Board time and energy may be consumed by schemes to keep the institution open rather than in planning program and meeting needs.

The Board must be clear that the institution exists to serve children and their families. This is the only justification for the existence of the institution; service must be the focus of the Board.

SUPPORTING CONSTITUENCY

Every agency has a supporting constituency. In some cases, the constituency is clearly defined: the agency may be sponsored by a fraternal organization, a service club, a religious denomination, a jurisdictional area of a religious denomination (e.g., a Presbyterian Synod, a United Methodist Conference, etc.), or some other discrete, identifiable entity. In other cases, the supporting constituency is not identifiable, but consists of groups or individuals who are interested in the agency, believe in its mission, and support its work.

Whichever the case, supporting constituents have a right to expect that their contributions will be used efficiently and effectively to carry out a stated purpose and that the affairs of the agency will be conducted in an ethical and professionally responsible manner.

A Board of Directors is established because it is manifestly impracticable for all supporting constituents to participate in agency operations. The Board operates in the place of, or on behalf of, those constituents; it performs the work which they would perform if logistically they could do so. The Board is, in effect, the alter ego of the supporting constituents.

MISSION STATEMENT

The Board develops a mission statement which declares the purpose for which the agency exists, defines the services it purports to offer, and identifies the clients it intends to serve. The mission statement should be couched in simple language which can be understood by anyone who might be interested in the agency or in its program.

The mission statement is the guide for the Board. When a new program or new service is suggested, the controlling question is, "Does this fit into the mission of the agency?"

The mission statement may be changed from time to time, but until it is changed, all programs and services, all acquisitions of property, all hiring of new staff should pass scrutiny as to whether or not the addition or change will support the basic mission of the agency as defined in its mission statement.

LONG-RANGE PLANNING

Long-range planning is specifically the responsibility of the Board. The Board should constantly look one year, five years, ten years into the future and set goals for the agency.

Goals may appropriately be set for financial development, program development, board organization and recruitment, physical plant improvement, equipment renewal, staff recruitment and training, addition of staff, etc. Once a goal has been achieved, it ceases to be a goal, and a replacement goal must be developed.

A Board is well advised to have sequential plans for development, with one-year, five-year, and ten-year plans. Short-range goals, that is, one- or two-year goals, should be reviewed at each Board meeting to see whether or not progress is being made to achieve the goals. When a plan for five years or more has been adopted by the Board, it should be reviewed at least annually to assess progress and to make modifications where necessary.

Goals cannot properly be set only in terms of what services the agency wishes to offer. Part of the goal-setting task is awareness of the needs of the community served by the agency. The services offered by the agency must be related to the need for those services and to the services which are offered by other agencies.

The "community served by the agency" may be defined in various ways: it can be defined in geographic terms—the city, county, or state in which the agency is located; it can be defined in service terms, e.g., delinquent adolescents, unwed parents, neglected/dependent children, children awaiting adoption; or some more specialized definition may be necessary, e.g., some denominational agencies still serve only members of their sponsoring denomination. However the community is defined, the institution's program should address the needs of that community, and the services of all agencies serving that community should have some coherence and communication.

A long-range planning committee will take service needs into account when developing a long-range plan. This means that the Board must make an assessment of community needs and the resources which are available to meet those needs.

The United Way, local and state departments of social services, local and state departments of mental health, city and county probation departments, the department of youth services, the school system, and other child-caring institutions will be helpful in identifying needs and resources. Statistical data are helpful; interviews with purchasers of services and with officials, supervisors, and workers of the aforementioned departments and agencies can give the Board guidance in planning.

Part of the long-range planning responsibility is keeping in touch with trends. The program which is needed and appropriate today may well be outdated in five years. The needs of the community may have changed; insights into how best to serve children and their families will have improved; additional agencies may have been organized and new services provided; some services may have disappeared; or for other reasons there may no longer be a market for the services which are provided today. Flexibility must be a part of Board planning.

The Board should view the program as a vital, living response to human needs. As needs change, the program changes. Too often, a Board and the administration develop one program and keep it unchanged from year to year. Whatever the needs, the program should be in constant process of evolving.

Long-Range planning means, in part, anticipating when services need to be changed. One of the advantages of a private agency is that it can respond more readily to changing needs than a public agency. In a private agency, the Board of Directors can change the mission statement, the staffing pattern, the program, or anything else about the agency. A public agency is created by legislature, and program change and budgeting must go through the whole legislative process. Change there is possible, but it is a more cumbersome procedure.

The committee which is responsible for long-range planning should document its findings, date them, note the sources of its information, and should seek constantly to update its information.

BUDGET

Providing the funds to support the program is specifically a Board responsibility. The Board is responsible for the agency; therefore, the Board is responsible for providing the funds to operate the agency.

The executive director cannot administer the program and simultaneously raise sufficient funds to keep the agency in operation, nor should he be expected to do so. The executive director may be helpful to the Board in a tangential way in raising funds, but his job is to administer program. Responsibility for providing income belongs to the Board.

The Board's financial responsibility can be discharged in a variety of ways: the Board can negotiate with the state Department of Social Services or other placing agencies for purchase-of-service fees; it can request inclusion in the United Fund; it can seek increased support from the sponsoring organization; the Board can seek support from foundations and endowments; it can hire a fund-raiser; it can establish a memorial gift program; it can pay for the program out of its own pockets; or it can fulfill its responsibility to provide operating funds in other ways.

Endowment

In long-range terms, the most effective method of agency support is an endowment.

An endowment is money that is invested in a permanent fund for the purpose of earning interest. The endowment principle is never touched; only the interest is used for operating expenses.

Although interest on an endowment varies from year to year, an endowment provides dependable income, and thus ensures continuity of the agency and of the program. An endowment provides a base for budget-making.

Purchase of Service Fees

Many agencies require or accept purchase of service fees for children who are placed by public departments or other placing agencies. The Board should be aware that public policy changes, and public monies available for purchase of services vary with changes in federal and state administrations. The agency which depends entirely or in large part upon public money for operating expenses is vulnerable to such changes, which may require curtailing or eliminating programs or, in extreme cases, eliminate the agency.

Some Boards limit the proportion of operating funds which can come from public sources; for example, they mandate that no more than one-third or one-fourth of the operating budget will consist of public monies; the remainder must come from private sources.

Other agencies use their own funds to operate the basic program and use public monies only for additions to the program, such as special teachers, a staff psychologist, an experimental program, etc.

In either case, if public funds should be eliminated, the existence of the agency is not at risk; the basic program continues.

Fund-Raising

Various methods of raising funds are used. (See "Development Committee," Chapter 5.)

Part of fund-raising is public relations, making sure that the public knows about the agency and what it does. Raising money for the care of children is relatively easy, for the general public has an instinctive concern for children in need. They must be informed of the need, however, and they must be assured that the program is worthy of their support.

Unfortunately, raising money for buildings or other physical assets is always easier than raising money to pay the food bill, fuel bill, or light bill. Donors tend to like to have brass plaques placed on their gifts. Education of supporting constituents with respect to the agency's range of needs is the only way to overcome this very human tendency.

Whatever the means, providing the income to operate the agency remains a Board responsibility.

USE OF AGENCY ASSETS

The Board is legally and morally responsible for the agency, both for the program and for the use of its assets. There is some legal question at the moment as to whether or not a religious denomination can be sued with respect to the affairs of one of its subordinate agencies. There is no doubt, however, about whether or not Board members can be sued — they can be. Thus, it is a matter of some urgency that Board business be conducted in an orderly manner, with scrupulous care being taken with regard to agency affairs.

The Board ensures that agency assets are used judiciously and that they are used for the purpose for which they were designed or donated. This involves a variety of activities such as, but not limited to, the following: installing a dependable accounting system; ensuring that preventive maintenance is used for all buildings and equipment; checking on the use of agency vehicles, which are intended for agency use, not personal use; guaranteeing that a gift given for a specific purpose is used for that purpose only; requiring that comparative shopping is used for minor items and that competitive bids are secured for major purchases; making sure that the agency farm makes money or, if it loses money, that it makes a significant enough contribution to the program that it is worth operating, etc.

Too often, irregularities are uncovered only in the midst of a crisis, when major mismanagement is discovered. Such an event reflects directly upon Board members and the work of the Board.

The Board will have liability insurance for Board members and for staff members. Liability insurance is not easy to find, but it can be found. A knowledgeable insurance agent is helpful in locating adequate insurance coverage.

Bad news travels fast. Maintaining a reputation for integrity is simpler than regaining it, once it has been lost.

ACCOUNTABILITY OF FUNDS AND PROPERTY

The Board must account for the use of gifts and other assets of the agency. Integrity of the Board and the staff must be above reproach if donations are to continue. Without being unduly cynical, it must be said that integrity of the staff cannot be assumed by the Board. Checks and balances must be established by which the Board can document that funds and property are properly used and accounted for. Periodic, thorough examination must be made of the use of funds, property, and other assets.

The Board contracts for an annual audit by an independent auditing firm, one unrelated to any member of the staff or of the Board. Careful instructions must be given to the auditors so that they understand the intent of the Board with respect to accounting, reimbursements, and other areas which may be maintained in a slipshod manner, if not the subject of outright abuse. Attention must be given also to the disclaimer which routinely appears at the beginning of the auditor's report, which may inadvertently conceal the possibility of poor administrative practice. The accountant on the Board can interpret this disclaimer.

Proper accountability of the use of agency assets emerges primarily out of effective committee work, of which more will be said later. If committees have an adequate grasp of their work assignment, the likelihood of misuse of property, whether deliberate or accidental, is diminished.

Accountability is specifically a Board responsibility.

POLICIES

The Board develops two kinds of policies: by-laws which govern the work of the Board, and program policies, which govern the work of the administration.

By-laws provide orderly procedures through which Board work is conducted. Like all procedures, they need updating from time to time. At least every five years, by-laws should be reviewed carefully and brought up to date.

Program policies define the parameters of agency service within the mission statement and establish the framework within which staff operate.

The parameters of agency service are set forth in a statement of the clients which the agency will be served; for example, "The agency will accept boys and girls ages 12-17 who have been adjudged delinquent; the maximum length of stay is 24 months."

Personnel policies set by the Board will include, but are not limited to, employment benefits, vacations, grievance procedures, salary scale, emergency leave, unpaid leave, job descriptions, and all related matters.

As a practical matter, organization of Board documents is facilitated if each Board member is provided with a large, three-ring notebook. The notebook should contain dividers labeled for at least the following kinds of documents:

- Board membership list, giving names, addresses, telephone numbers, and committee assignments
- Board minutes
- By-laws
- Personnel manual
- Job descriptions
- One divider for each committee
- Correspondence
- Miscellaneous

If all Board communications are dated and reproduced on punched paper, the Board member can file it immediately in its proper place, thus having an organized, compact file when attending to Board business. Many Board members do not have a file cabinet at home, and the usual alternative to having a notebook is to have Board papers variously lost in desk drawers, magazine racks, accidentally thrown out with old mail and newspapers, and located in other obscure places all of which defeat attempts at organization. Notebooks for all Board members, identically organized, facilitate Board work.

ADMINISTRATIVE STRUCTURE

The Board does not administer the agency; rather, the Board provides the policies and framework within which the agency can be administered and then hires an administrator to carry out the policies.

From that point on, the Board erects a mechanism by which it is assured that its framework remains intact, but it allows the executive director freedom within that framework and does not interfere with his work.

Normally the administrator designs a staffing pattern which would be adequate to fulfill the agency mission and submits that plan for Board approval. The Board approves whatever plan it feels is satisfactory and establishes the positions called for by the plan. The Board supports the administrator and works closely with him, but it will not take administrative duties upon itself.

The executive director's first responsibility is to the here-and-now. What is the program design, how well is the program functioning, how adequate is the staff, how effective is his administration in carrying out the mandate of the Board, what problems exist, how adequately does the budget provide for a professional program of child care, etc. Secondarily, he has a responsibility to the agency's future.

The Board has a dual focus: the present and the future. The Board must be constantly vigilant that present program, policies, facilities, and finances are in good order and that they support the agency mission and the future direction of the agency. Their next concern is how the Board can support and facilitate the work of the executive director.

Once concerns for the present have been taken care of, the Board is concerned about the future. The essential task of the Board is to envision what will be happening in one year, five years, and ten years, to set goals for the future, and to determine how those goals are supported by what is transpiring today. The Board focuses on the long-range picture, the overall goals and performance of the agency, its support, and the use of its assets. The Board must guard against becoming mired in inconsequential details or issues, and also against usurping administrative prerogatives. The Board's responsibility is policy; the executive director's responsibility is administration.

The Board must be proactive with respect to monitoring the program, the property, the finances, and the executive director's job performance. If it fails to be proactive, the Board will become reactive, usually after disaster has struck. The Board meeting is no place for assumptions; the Board must have facts. The Board makes decisions based on reports from the several committees and from the executive director.

EXECUTIVE DIRECTOR

The executive director is delegated those duties which the Board cannot discharge: the daily implementation of program. The hiring of an executive director is a major task of the Board. The qualifications and hiring process will be discussed later.

The executive director is expected to have more extensive knowledge and experience in professional child care than the Board needs, but the Board must have a sufficient base of knowledge to have meaningful discussions with the executive. Through reasoned discussions, the idealism of the executive director and the realism of the Board can find a meeting ground.

No Board should put itself in the position of following an executive director blindly. The Board cannot hire an executive director and then turn the agency over to him to run. The role of the executive director and the role of the Board are complementary; they are the two parts of a whole. Together, the Board and the executive director constitute the team which will serve children and their families.

The Board has every right to expect the executive director to demonstrate and document that he is functioning within the framework established by the Board. As long as the executive director operates in accordance with the Board's instructions, the Board will do everything possible to support the executive director. At any time, however, that the executive director fails to adhere to the Board's direction, the Board must wield its power to get things back in line.

The line between Board responsibilities and administrative responsibilities must be kept clear.

PROGRAM OF EXCELLENCE

The Board must ensure that a problem of excellence is maintained.

While it is true that Board members are not expected to become experts in residential care, it is equally true that the Board must maintain an awareness of and contact with the field of professional child care. The Board must have some reference point for considering program issues.

The program must respond to today's needs and reflect current professional thinking. Whether that awareness and contact come through consultation, through having several residential care professionals on the Board, through visiting other agencies, or through some other means is immaterial. The crucial factor is that the focus of the Board be riveted to providing professional service to children and their families and that it have some understanding of what constitutes such service.

Boards frequently do not involve themselves in a substantive way with professional considerations. Too often they have not kept up with advances in the field of professional child care, with the result that their program provides answers to questions which are no longer being asked; provides services which are no longer needed, and operates essentially as it was ten or twenty years ago. Some Board members have their own intransigent ideas about institutional care and choose to set their own pattern of institutional life irrespective of professional considerations.

The uninformed Board is unable relate to professional and program issues raised by the executive director; it is unable to raise pertinent questions with the administration with respect to program. The uninformed Board has little choice but to accept the counsel of the executive director.

Part II of this book presents some basic concepts of child care with which every Board member should be familiar.

PROPERTY

Property is in large measure the least important part of an agency's operation, but many Boards get hung up on property and spend on physical matters uncounted hours which could more profitably be spent on other matters.

Some Board members and some supporting constituents equate elegance of property with excellence of program. This is in error; the two are totally unrelated. The issues to be considered with respect to property are adequacy, safety, convenience, and cleanliness. An excellent program of child care can be operated in a barn, if staff are trained and caring. We do not want children to live in a barn, but better to live in a barn with a good program than in a palace with no program. Elegance of property is part of the adult value system; children in residence do not care about elegance, and their parents may be intimidated by elegance.

Just as constituents prefer to give to tangible things like buildings, it is easier for Board members to deal with buildings, which are tangible, than with program, which is intangible. More Board members have had experience with buildings than with program, and they may be more comfortable dealing with the tangible. Additionally, Board members may think that the quality of the physical facility indicates the effectiveness of the Board. The question with respect to buildings is adequacy, not elegance.

One point should be made clearly. Occasionally a Board or an executive director will deliberately keep the property looking like something out of Charles Dickens on the theory that people will "feel sorry" for the agency and therefore will be prompted to give more money. This is a fallacy.

People want to give to organizations which clearly are prosperous and are cared about; they want to take pride in that to which they have given their money. This is especially true of people who are capable of giving large gifts, who know the value of property. They know that maintaining property in presentable condition is less expensive than restoring it after it has deteriorated; they are disenchanted by an agency which is rundown or shabby in appearance; they are aware that the appearance of property indicates the quality of stewardship being exercised. It is natural for them to assume that any of their gifts will be treated with the same care as the property has received, and they will be less likely to make major donations to a facility that is decrepit in appearance.

The Board will, of course, provide the best property which the budget will permit. No one need be apologetic about old buildings, however, provided they are maintained and kept attractive. Adequate maintenance will keep old buildings serviceable for many years. An architect or engineer should be employed to determine when a building appears to have outlived its usefulness and when replacement might be better stewardship than repair or restoration.

Every budget should have a maintenance and replacement item, for children appropriately referred to institutions today tend to have destructive tendencies when they arrive.

Inside the buildings, furnishings should be whole, not have rips or tears; broken furniture should be repaired if it cannot be replaced; carpets should be in one piece and clean. Decorations should be appropriate to the age of the children in residence.

Board members should give some attention to the general climate of the cottages. A cottage in which children live should look as if children live there. Furniture arranged in stiff, geometric patterns, rooms without books or magazines, wall decorations suitable for another era, or rooms that are maintained with operating-room sterility indicate to the visitor that children have a low priority. Inexpensive pictures and posters which are age-appropriate for the children in the cottage can brighten otherwise dull or dark rooms. Books and magazines should be in evidence. Furniture that is comfortable for children and arranged casually indicate that children live there.

Children should be allowed to decorate their own rooms. If posters or pictures cannot be mounted on the wall, each child should have a large bulletin board where he can mount whatever he wants to. Appearance should never take precedence over the welfare of the residents.

Board members are not to be involved in housekeeping; that is an administrative concern. Cottage life should not be turned topsy turvy because Board members are on campus; child care workers should not live in fear of an unexpected visit to the cottage by a Board member. An unmade bed, a cluttered living room, or a sink full of unwashed dishes is not a proper concern for a Board member. The child care worker is responsible for housekeeping standards, and he may have a valid reason for permitting the apparent disorder. The child care worker is responsible to the administration, not to the Board.

THE INDIVIDUAL BOARD MEMBER

The individual Board member must take Board duties seriously. The individual Board member has certain responsibilities, such as the following:

1. Prepare for and attend committee meetings and Board meetings. The Board member will study and analyze in advance reports and recommendations and come to the meeting prepared to discuss the reports and recommendations. The Board member will bring his best insights to the work of the committee and of the Board.

2. Learn the by-laws of the Board. Each Board member is responsible for adhering to by-laws and for ensuring that the Board as a whole follows its own by-laws.

3. Learn the program of the agency. "Learning the program" includes knowing the needs which the program seeks to meet, the constraints under which the program operates, the methods used to meet needs, etc.

Know the child welfare system of the community. What are the needs of the community, and how does this agency fit into the constellation of services in the community?

After a year of Board membership, the Board member should be able to interpret the agency accurately. Part of the responsibility of

Board membership is representing the agency in public relations presentations.

4. Contribute financially to the agency as one's personal situation permits.

5. Look for ways for the Board and the agency to save money. The Board member's community contacts may effect savings in purchases; the timing or nature of purchases may need to be questioned; alternative, less expensive, ways of accomplishing a task should be considered. The list of possibilities for saving money is endless.

One strange quirk of human nature requires constant vigilance by the Board. There is a qualitative difference in using one's own property and using property that belongs to someone else, especially when that property belongs to an agency. Subconsciously, one tends to think that agency funds are more plentiful than personal funds, and that less care is needed with agency property than with one's own.

More than one executive director or staff member has fallen into the temptation of feathering his own nest at agency expense or in overlooking ways of preserving property or of saving money because the property and the money belongs to an agency. Personal gas tanks have been filled at agency pumps; agency hay has appeared in staff members' barns; residents have been paid by the agency to improve staff members' private property; executives have granted themselves and favored staff members salary increases unbeknownst to the Board; legitimate expense accounts have had illegitimate billings, etc.

Most of these people are not basically dishonest; they are simply human and somewhat self-centered, and they have sacrificed the good of the agency for their own personal gain.

It is specifically the responsibility of Board members to safeguard the assets of the organization and to forestall or at least to identify and correct such abuses.

6. Maintain a healthy skepticism and inquisitiveness about all aspects of Board and agency functioning. Do not assume anything. Just because a Board president or an executive director or someone else in an official position says that something is so does not necessarily make it so. Check, double-check, and check again.

7. Do not be intimidated by anyone. Some Board members or staff members are very persuasive; others have booming voices; still others are accustomed to commanding, and the air of confidence they exude deludes one into thinking that what they say must be true. Look behind

the external characteristics and analyze what is being said. Ask questions and stick with those questions until a reasonable answer is produced. Do not be embarrassed at not having information; there is no such thing as a stupid question. Any question which honestly seeks information is legitimate.

8. Ensure that the power of the Board is exerted as a whole. If the authority of the Board is being monopolized by a few members, or if the executive committee is usurping or has been given the authority of the Board, bring this to the attention of the Board, and keep this issue alive until it is resolved. The Board member holds a position of trust; he is not in a popularity contest.

9. Work in a teamwork relationship with other Board members. Insist that other Board members also work in a teamwork relationship.

10. Never give up the struggle to improve services for children and their families.

SUMMARY OF BOARD RESPONSIBILITIES

The Board's responsibilities are very specific: the Board of Trustees is totally responsible for the agency, including its function, its assets, and its performance. In practical terms, the Board of Directors is responsible for the physical property, the policies, the program, the budget, and the executive director.

In pursuit of its responsibilities, the Board focuses on the long-range picture, the overall goals and performance of the agency. Because, like supporting constituents, all Board members cannot be present in the agency on a daily basis to operate the agency, the Board hires an executive director to carry out the detail work — to administer the policies which the Board has established. The executive director, in turn, hires other staff to carry out the details of his task.

Because the Board is responsible for the agency, it must be strong in its own work, and it *must* retain control of the agency. This means, among other things, that it must develop and adhere to policies, procedures, and time frames which will enable the Board to plan adequately, ensure that fiscal responsibility is achieved, that responsible stewardship to its supporting constituents is maintained, and that the agency's work is being accomplished in accordance with the Board's wishes.

The Board will distinguish between Board responsibilities and administrative responsibilities; it will faithfully discharge Board responsibilities, and it will refrain from interfering with administrative responsibilities.

The Board is a constant in the life of the agency. Executive directors and other staff members come and go, but the Board remains, and it provides underlying stability and continuity for the agency. Therefore, the Board must be in control and must know what it is doing.

Chapter 2

BOARD ORGANIZATION

MEMBERS of a volunteer Board cannot devote full time, or even a major amount of time, to Board activities; therefore, the Board must be organized in such a way and develop procedures which will enable it to work most efficiently and most effectively. Talents and skills of all Board members must be utilized in the service of Board work.

BOARD COMPOSITION

The Board should have a representative cross section of the supporting constituency, the needs of the agency, consumers, and the society in which the agency operates. These factors are not mutually exclusive, but attention should be given to ensure representation of each.

The prudent Board identifies the kinds of skills needed on the Board and the groups which logically should be represented and then seeks for Board membership individuals who possess those skills or who represent those groups.

For the business of the Board, skills of the following are helpful:

Accountant
Contractor/architect/builder
Businesspersons, especially those who operate their own businesses.
Officers of industry/corporations
Investment specialist/broker
Professional in out-of-home care of children
Judge, especially one who handles juvenile or family cases
Attorney
Physician
Personnel manager
Someone skilled in public relations/media

Some Boards need members with other specific skills. If the agency owns a farm, someone experienced in farming matters is needed; if the agency owns forest land, someone skilled in forest management is appropriate; if the agency owns property which has oil or gas deposits, someone knowledgeable about mineral leases should be included. Some agencies have other, unique needs.

In addition to specific expertise, the following should be represented:

Geographic areas in which supporting constituents live
Ethnic minorities
High society/wealth
Educators
Consumers of the agency's services

Consumer representation on the Board may be in the form of a former resident or client, the family of a client, someone who is employed by an agency which refers children for care, e.g., state department of social services, or someone in another position which represents users of the services offered. The principle is to have represented the viewpoint and experience of those who actually use, or have used, the services.

A word about the expertise of Board members. A Board member is not expected to conduct free for the agency the business which is his livelihood. Thus, a Board member who is an attorney is not expected to conduct all agency legal business free of charge; rather, he is expected to advise the Board as to when legal assistance is needed and how best to have legal matters taken care of. A Board member who is a physician or dentist is not expected to provide medical care or dental care for children in residence. He is expected to advise with respect to the design of the medical or dental program for residents; he may be asked to help the Board or administration interpret the recommendation of a local physician or dentist, such as a recommendation for orthodontia.

After a Board has specified the talents or skills which are most needful for its business, nominations should ensure that those talents are always available. For example, when an accountant is due to rotate off the Board, a new Board member with accounting expertise should be recruited.

Corporations frequently loan employees for Board membership as a part of the corporation's contribution to a community. A Board may approach a corporation to ask for an accountant or a person with other specific skills to serve on the Board. This approach has a double advantage: the Board acquires the talents needed; board membership becomes part of that employee's duties, hence there is no question about his being able to attend Board meetings during normal working hours.

The sponsoring organization or the by-laws of some Boards mandate Board membership for specified persons. For example, a denominationally-sponsored agency may require that a given proportion of Board members be members of the clergy. Care should be taken to balance the remainder of the Board.

SIZE OF BOARD

The size of the Board is determined to some degree upon the size of the agency and the scope of its operations. The Board should be as large as necessary, but as small as possible. The Board should have sufficient members to staff committees adequately and to have diversity of qualifications of Board members, but not so many as to make Board meetings unwieldy or difficult to convene. The larger the Board, the more difficult it is to have full attendance at Board meetings.

For most agencies, a Board of from 18 to 36 members is adequate. A 30-member Board can have five standing committees of six members each without duplication of committee membership. For most agencies, this should be sufficient.

All Board work should be vested in a single Board. In the past, some agencies have had a multiple-board arrangement, with a men's board and a women's board, or a board of trustees in charge of property and finance and a general board for program, personnel, and policy, or with some other division of labor. Multiple boards complicate the execution of Board responsibilities; prompt and accurate communication between or among boards and coordination of the work of the several Boards are difficult to achieve.

One variation which has been used successfully is to have an Auxiliary Board or an Advisory Board. Such Boards have a discrete purpose which is helpful, but these Boards have no authority over administration or program.

The Auxiliary Board typically raises money for specific projects, such as building construction or renovation, educational scholarships, support of a specialized staff member, etc.

The Advisory Board typically provides professional expertise, a wider range of community representation than is possible within Board membership, or other specialized functions.

BY-LAWS

By-laws are the directives for Board organization and activity. All of the business of the Board is directed by the by-laws.

By-laws state how many members the Board will have, how Board members are to be elected, what officers the Board will have, what their term of office is, and what their responsibilities are.

By-laws establish committees, state committee assignments, and indicate how committee chairpersons will be elected or appointed.

By-laws state how the business of the Board will be conducted, most often prescribing Roberts' Rules of Order as the pattern.

By-laws contain a procedure for by-law amendment, because by-laws become out-dated. Periodically, at least every five years, an *adhoc* committee should be appointed to review the by-laws in detail and to make recommendations to the Board for appropriate changes. Until the by-laws are amended, however, they are to be followed carefully. As with other aspects of agency operation, lawsuits may hinge on whether or not official procedures were followed.

FREQUENCY OF MEETINGS

Board meetings are convened for the purpose of making decisions. The information upon which the decisions are based cannot be generated in the Board meeting itself, but is generated by committees in advance of the Board meeting. More about committees later.

A maximum of four meetings per year should be adequate for the Board, provided committees are active and provided adequate preparation is made for the Board meeting.

Boards which meet more frequently than quarterly tend to have less well-organized meetings; preparation tends to be less adequate; more time is spent conducting less business, and it is easy to use the whole Board to perform committee work, which is both ineffective and a misuse of Board time.

TERM OF OFFICE

Effective Board work is time- and energy-consuming. Many persons who are excellent Board members cannot devote endless years of volunteer time to the work of one Board; they may be willing to give their energies to Board work for a specified period of time. Thus, most Board have a limited term of membership, frequently three years.

Additionally, many Boards provide for rotating terms of office, with one-third of the Board members being elected each year for a three-year term. In this manner, one-third of the Board members are new; one-third have one year of experience, and one-third have two years of experience.

Such Boards frequently require that after completing two terms, a Board member must go off the Board for at least one year before becoming eligible for reelection. This excellent system provides for automatic infusion of new ideas into Board work, and it painlessly eliminates from the Board those members who turn out to be inactive or who have had gradually diminished interest in or time for Board work. Productive Board members can be reelected to the Board after one year.

New ideas are important to Board work. Everyone develops his own patterns of thinking and acting; the unchanged Board does the same. After two consecutive terms, most Board members have made their maximum contribution to the Board, and replacement is appropriate.

A Board cannot function effectively with erratic attendance by Board members. By-laws of some agencies include a provision that three successive, unexcused absences from Board meetings constitute automatic resignation from the Board. The by-laws also provide a mechanism by which Board members who have resigned can be replaced.

BOARD MEMBER RECRUITMENT

When persons have been identified who have talents or skills which would be helpful to the Board, before they are asked to commit themselves, they should given a clear idea of what their contribution is expected to be and of the time involvement in Board membership.

Four Board meetings and four committee meetings per year are standard, minimum expectations. In addition, the Board member is expected to spend time preparing for committee and Board meetings. Committee work may involve many hours of work apart from the committee meeting itself.

The candidate will have to decide for himself whether or not he can invest in Board work the amount of time required plus travel time. If he cannot, or chooses not to, commit herself to the minimum time requirements, in the interest of the Board's work the invitation should be declined or withdrawn. Attendance at Board meetings and committee meetings must have a high priority for all Board members.

BOARD ORIENTATION

A separate day should be set aside for the orientation of new Board members. The orientation should take place on the agency campus so that the new Board member may have a tour of the facilities. Orientation must include more than a tour, however.

Orientation may appropriately be divided into several parts: orientation to the field of institutional care in general and orientation to this agency in particular. On orientation day, Board members should have an opportunity to meet and converse informally with staff and, if appropriate, to meet some of the children in care.

The new Board member should be provided with program description, by-laws, and other pertinent documents in advance of the orientation day. Reading those documents in preparation for orientation will give a head start on understanding the agency, but it may also be confusing, since the new Board member may have no point of reference for his reading. The purpose of orientation is to make those documents come alive, to produce a beginning understanding of what the agency is all about, and to give a framework for beginning to understand the work of the Board.

Orientation deserves its own day. If orientation is made a part of a regular Board meeting, neither orientation nor Board meeting will be served well.

USE OF BOARD MEMBERS

Once recruited, Board members must be put to meaningful tasks. Effective Board work is the result of combining the insights, experience, and energy of all Board members. Each Board member was recruited for some talent, characteristic, expertise, capability, or constituency, and those qualities should be fully utilized.

To recruit a Board member for some talent and then not to use that talent is an insult. People who are interested in the agency's work and commit their time to Board work expect their membership to count for something. Board members are competent in their own fields, they know competency when they see it, and they expect competence in Board administration. No one wants to be a figurehead, a token, or a symbol, nor does a person qualified for Board membership have time to waste on tokenism.

Simply attending Board meetings and voting on issues is not acceptable to the capable Board member. The Board which permits this superficial type of Board membership will find that valuable Board members resign, and the work increasingly devolves upon a few Board members. Perhaps one of the most common weaknesses of Boards is at this point.

The Board must find the time and the mechanism for drawing out the best that is in each Board member and putting that best to work in the service of the agency. This is accomplished most effectively through committee work.

Board officers and committee chairpersons should be especially mindful of the personalities of Board members. Where some Board member unintentionally dominates discussion because of an inherently assertive personality, a booming voice, or some other personal mannerism, and some other Board member is reticent and does not participate because of inherent shyness or because of being easily intimidated, the Board officer or committee chairperson must find a means to equalize the contribution of these Board members. Disparate personal characteristics must be accommodated. The contribution of each is valued, deserves equal consideration, and must be utilized.

In most cases, disuse of available talents is the result of ineffective board organization or insensitivity in the conduct of a meeting. In some Boards, however, disuse of talents has been the design of a few persons who wish to dominate Board work. Usurpation of the rights of Board members by a few should not be tolerated.

The by-laws state how committee chairman are elected or appointed. Here again, due consideration must be given to the personality of the prospective committee chairman. The chairman must have skills in group leadership; he must be able to capitalize upon both the professional expertise and the personalities of committee members and to motivate and lead them in the committee task.

COMMITTEE ASSIGNMENTS

Board members generally will be assigned to committees in accordance with their specific talents or expressed interest. Thus, the accountant will become a member of the Finance Committee, the mechanic and the contractor will become members of the Buildings, Grounds, and Equipment Committee, the representative of the Department of Social Services will join the Program Committee, etc.

Another factor which will influence committee assignments is the personalities of Board members. In making committee assignments, the Board President will make a conscious decision of whether to staff one committee with all dominant personalities, all passive personalities, or to have a mix.

The composition of the committee will also depend to some degree upon the personality of the committee chairman. A chairman who is inherently of a shy or retiring nature may have difficulty leading a committee which includes one or more dominant types.

No rule of thumb is possible; these are factors to be considered when establishing committee assignments in order to make maximum use of Board members' talents and skills and to provide the best possible counsel for the Board.

One other factor which may play into committee assignment is geography. If Board membership is drawn from across a state or from a larger area, in order to facilitate the convening of committees, committee assignments may be made according to the geographic location of Board members. Thus, Finance Committee members may be located in the southeast quadrant of the state, Program Committee members in the northwest quadrant, etc. In large states, much travel time can be eliminated with this plan, and committee attendance may be better. Geographic location may be an additional factor in identifying candidates for Board membership. Geographic considerations may not always be realistic either for selecting Board members or making committee assignment, but the possibility should be borne in mind.

Any procedure which will enhance committee and Board participation and attendance should be considered.

REIMBURSEMENT OF BOARD MEMBERS

Board members should be reimbursed for their expenses in attending Board and committee meetings, long-distance telephone calls, and for any other expenses incurred in Board work. The purpose of reimbursement is to ensure that no one is prohibited from becoming a Board member because of the expense involved.

All Board members should be requested to turn in expense accounts, irrespective of whether or not they need the money. Full documentation must be made of Board expenses for the purpose of calculating accurately the next year's budget. The Board cannot know from one year to the next which Board members wish, or can afford, to pay their own expenses, and it must budget full expenses for every Board member. If a Board member does not wish to accept money from the agency, he may endorse the check and send it back to the agency.

Reimbursement rates should be realistic in today's economy, but Board members should not expect to live in luxury simply because they can turn in an expense account. A maximum rate for motels and meals is necessary; the Board member may exceed the reimbursement rates if he wishes to, but he knows in advance how much will be reimbursed.

Reimbursement rates for Board members should be identical to reimbursement rates for staff members. If reimbursement rates for staff members are inadequate for Board members, very likely they are inadequate also for staff members. Dual standards suggest that staff members are second-class citizens and are a sure cause of resentment.

Chapter 3

THE EXECUTIVE DIRECTOR

FUNCTION OF THE EXECUTIVE DIRECTOR

THE EXECUTIVE DIRECTOR is the employee of the Board. He is hired for only one reason: to implement the Board's will. He functions within the framework and in accordance with the policies established by the Board. He acts only in those areas to which the Board has assigned him. All of his work is subject to scrutiny by the Board to ensure that he remains within that framework and that he functions in accordance with Board policies. The Board justifiably expects from the executive director loyalty to the agency, its mission, and to the Board. Conversely, the executive director justifiably expects loyalty and support from the Board.

HIRING AN EXECUTIVE DIRECTOR

The Board should seek the best-qualified person available to be executive director. Most states' minimum licensing standards for institutions establish a range of education and/or experience which is acceptable for an executive director of a licensed institution. By design, minimum standards are exactly that—minimum. The lowest permissible qualifications are generally inadequate for today's institutional climate and clientele, which require more than minimum knowledge, experience, and skill. The prudent Board will eliminate from its thinking the lower allowable levels of education and experience and seek a candidate who is thoroughly qualified both by training and experience for the task. A properly qualified candidate will exceed minimum permissible standards.

The selection of an executive director is a major function of the Board. The selection process should not be hurried; ample time should be allowed to develop a list of candidates and then to check references, to have extended discussions with each of the candidates, to ask questions and to answer their questions.

The selection process starts with advertising the availability of the position. Advertising through professional journals and denominational publications (for those agencies which are operated by religious denominations) and spreading the word to licensing representatives, associations of executives and social workers are just a few of the avenues by which candidates may be identified.

When the list has been reduced to the two or three most likely-looking candidates, those persons should be brought at agency expense for interviews, to meet the Board, for a familiarization tour of agency property and program, and for interviews with staff and residents.

Pertinent information on the Board and Board goals, the agency mission, the program, budget, finances, the professional network within which the agency functions, and any licensing and/or consultation reports should be shared with the candidates. The candidates should be given as full and accurate information about the agency as is possible. Concealing pertinent information from candidates is unfair and casts aspersion on the integrity of the Board.

Similarly, the Board should ascertain the candidate's goals and professional interest, as well as reviewing in detail his credentials, training, experience, and success.

In other words, the candidating process seeks to establish demonstrated competence of the candidate and mutuality of professional interest and compatibility between candidate and Board. Both professional competence and compatibility with the Board are crucial. Candor on both sides is essential.

Before hiring, at least a second visit by the leading candidate is advisable. Both Board and candidate need time to reflect on first impressions, to digest information, and to identify and formulate questions or concerns.

Staff should have an opportunity to interact with the candidate, for their jobs and the climate within which they are expected to work are at stake. Residents also should have an opportunity to interact with the candidate, for their lives, too, will be directly affected by the new executive director. Residents have a perspective which Board members cannot have, and they may pick up clues with respect to the candidate, either positive or negative, which the Board would not. Staff members and residents should have an opportunity to give their impressions of the candidate to the Board or Board committee; their impressions and reactions of both staff and residents may be helpful to the Board in developing an overall understanding of the candidate and his suitability for the position. The final decision, of course, remains with the Board.

The Board has four primary tools by which its work is accomplished: Board committees, the budget, the Board meeting, and the executive director. The Board should not feel that its work is finished when an executive director has been hired. When an executive director has been hired, only that portion of its work which relates to providing an executive director has been concluded. An unspoken part of the agreement in hiring an executive director is that once he has been hired, the Board will make every effort to support him in his work, which is distinctively the work of the Board.

HIRING CONDITIONS

The executive director should have a job description and a written contract. The job description specifies the duties; the contract specifies salary and benefits and provides the assurance of job security which is necessary for effective work.

The initial contract may appropriately be for one year, which serves in effect as a probationary period, a period in which the executive director and the Board develop a working relationship and explore their mutual compatibility. Subsequent contracts normally will be for three- or five-year periods.

The pay and benefits of the executive director should be commensurate with his responsibilities; they should also be equitable with the salaries of other staff members. Staff morale is adversely affected by disproportionate salaries for agency executives. Direct-care staff who live and work with troubled children are not amused by $12,000 salaries when it is known that the executive director receives $40,000 or more plus more benefits than they receive. Salaries are supposedly confidential; however, there are no secrets on an institutional campus.

Both Board and executive director need regularly to review in systematic fashion their expectations, achievements, and experience together. In order to document that the executive director is functioning as expected, the contract mandates an evaluation of the executive director by the Board at specified intervals and provides for an evaluation more frequently, if needed. An evaluation will be made at least at the end of each contract period. Whenever any part of the executive director's work falls short of Board expectations, a written evaluation is appropriate.

The executive director's evaluation should be initiated by the Board and should be executed by the Board (or a Board committee) and the executive director jointly. The evaluation addresses only the duties which are listed in the job description plus additional assignments made by the Board and recorded in Board minutes. The board cannot assume that the executive director knows what the Board wants; the purpose of a job description is to specify what is expected.

As with evaluations of all staff, the completed evaluation form serves as a basis for discussion by Board and executive director of the evaluation. The executive director should have the prerogative of appending to the written evaluation a statement of elaboration or disagreement with part or all of the evaluation. A copy of the evaluation goes into the executive director's personnel file; he should also have a personal copy of the completed, signed evaluation.

The only thing worse than a poor evaluation is no evaluation. Every employee has a right to know objectively how he and his work are perceived by his administrative superiors. The conscientious executive spends considerable energy in recognizing efforts of his staff. The Board must take the initiative to do the same for the executive director.

Just as the executive director deserves documented reassurance when his work is satisfactory, he deserves appropriate notice when his work is unsatisfactory so that he can make necessary changes.

The executive director—or any other employee—cannot be fired if evaluations have been "average" or above. An employee can properly be fired only after written evaluations have identified an area or areas of unsatisfactory job performance, followed by a period in which an improvement could have been made but was not made. In addition to reflecting negatively upon the Board, violation of this principle may lead to a lawsuit. Even if unsuccessful, the lawsuit generates negative publicity which few agencies need.

The evaluation and firing processes which the Board Personnel Policies provide for employees protect employees from capriciousness on the part of supervisors or the executive director. The executive director deserves equal treatment by the Board. The only exception to this is conviction or admission of illegal, immoral, or unethical conduct. A charge of misconduct is not basis for firing. Everyone who is administratively superior to others is vulnerable to accusations by a disgruntled staff member. The Board must check such accusations carefully.

The executive director's contract should not be self-perpetuating or automatically renewable. Following the evaluation at the end of a contract period, the Board should vote on a new contract which will then be signed by the Board and by the executive director.

FUNCTION OF THE EXECUTIVE DIRECTOR

The Board sets policy; the executive director implements policy.

The executive director is responsible for operating the program which the Board wishes to operate. His responsibility is to use the agency's assets carefully to achieve the agency mission.

The executive director refers all matters of policy to the Board through whatever mechanism the Board devises; for example, he may be directed to refer an offer of a donation of property to the Property Committee, bequests to the Finance Committee, and fund-raising or other projects to the Development Committee. He does not have the prerogative of declining offers of major donations without guidance from the Board, nor does he have the prerogative of launching major new projects without prior Board knowledge and approval.

The executive director provides the operating details by which the program will be carried on. For example, the Board Personnel Policies prescribe the number of vacation days and sick days for staff and the holidays which will be observed by the agency. Those are policy decisions and, consequently, belong to the Board. To implement those policies, the executive director develops a time-keeping mechanism which maintains a record of sick days and vacation days taken by each staff member and a record of which employees worked on an agency holiday or other overtime and are entitled to overtime pay or compensatory time.

The executive director is responsible for hiring sufficient, qualified staff to carry on the agency's work. He cannot establish or eliminate staff positions without Board approval, but the Board will not seek to influence the selection of specific individuals to fill positions which have been properly established.

If an established position is left vacant for longer than the normal time required for recruitment, the executive director should share with the Board his rationale for leaving a position vacant. Without such rationale, the Board may reasonably conclude that the position is superfluous and may move to abolish the position.

With regard to the budget, the Board may give the executive director permission to function independently within the limitations of the approved budget, either with respect to a line item of the budget or with respect to the budget as a whole.

With respect to a line item, for example, assume that $5000 was authorized for new furniture and $5000 was budgeted for new office equipment. The price of the furniture totalled $7500. The executive director reduced the office equipment allocation by $2500 and increased the furniture allocation by $2500.

With respect to the total budget, the Board may authorize the executive director to alter line items in accordance with experience, provided the budget total is not exceeded. For example, one staff position was vacant for six weeks, resulting in a saving of salary and benefits. The executive director moved $2000 from the salary line to the new equipment line to purchase new equipment for the maintenance department. Line items were altered, but the budget total was unaffected. No Board action was required if the Board had authorized the executive director to make such changes within the budget total.

A limitation should be placed on individual expenditures which can be authorized by the executive director. Most Boards authorize the executive director to approve purchases within the budget up to a certain amount without prior Board approval, frequently either $500 or $1000. Even those expenditures, however, are subject to budget limitations. No purchase or expenditure which exceeds the budget can be made without prior Board approval whether or not the expenditure is legitimate and whether or not it is within allowable limits for the executive director.

Certain routine expenses may be exempt from this rule, e.g., the utility bill may exceed the authorized amount for a given month due to the seasonal demands for heating or air conditioning; the executive director has little control over the amount of the bill. The Board can issue a blanket authorization to pay such usual expenses irrespective of the amount. Specific bills which are subject to blanket authorization should be listed in Board minutes.

The Board should be aware that every executive director operates on the "get the camel's nose inside the tent" theory. Once the nose is inside, the full animal shortly follows. This is not a criticism; it is simply standard political procedure. The Board's responsibility is to determine whether or not overall agency functioning will be enhanced by ultimately having a camel inside the tent.

If the executive director's request can be honored and still remain within the budget *and* within the mission of the agency, fine. It needs to be said repeatedly, however, that all requests for expenditure must be measured against the mission of the agency and against the budget and income. With respect to any request from the executive director, the Board should ask "Why," "Why now," "Is there an alternative, less expensive way of accomplishing this?" *The Board must retain its option of saying,* "*No.*" The Board, not the executive director, is finally responsible for the agency.

The executive director is properly an *exofficio* member of all Board committees so that he can keep abreast of the Board's thinking and so that he can provide current information on agency operations, needs, and achievements. The work of committees will be discussed later.

The executive director and the Board must work together to maintain the division between policy and administration. Policy is a Board function; administration is the executive director's function. When either the Board or the executive director strays across the line, one must alert the other to what has happened.

EXECUTIVE DIRECTOR'S REPORTS

The Executive Director is required to report at specified intervals to the Board on the status of the agency and the agency program.

The Board has a right to expect a report which reflects accurately the state of the agency and its program. Some of the executive director's report will be positive; some of it will be negative. The reporting of problems or problems areas should not be construed necessarily to be a reflection on the executive director, for the agency operates in a complex society. When problems or problem areas are reported, the appropriate question is how the Board and executive director, working together, can solve the problem.

The Board depends upon the executive director for candid reporting, and the Board is rightfully concerned if the executive director reports only upon progress made and other positives. Rarely can an honest report by the executive director be totally positive.

The executive director, in turn, justifiably expects a reasonable hearing and consideration of his report by the Board. Too often the executive director's report is left until the end of the Board meeting, and he winds up with four minutes to give his report while Board members are putting on their coats. This is unfair to the executive director, to the Board, to the agency, and to the children in care. The candor of the executive director's report will be directly related to the support which the Board has given the executive director in the past.

The executive director's report should be listed early in the agenda and given full consideration. The Board may request that the executive director provide copies of his report so that Board members can receive the report visually as well as orally.

BOARD SAFEGUARD

The Board expects the executive director to perform his duties in a professionally responsible and ethical manner. The prudent Board, however, will provide checks and balances by which it will be alerted to any situation which is not in accord with Board policy or wishes and which may require investigation. Although the executive director is responsible for the day-by-day affairs of the agency, the Board must maintain a proactive stance with regard to the agency. Ultimate responsibility for the agency belongs to the Board, which cannot afford to turn its responsibilities over to the executive director.

EXECUTIVE DIRECTOR TITLE

In recent years, the chief executive officer of a children's institution has been called "executive director"; earlier titles were "administrator" or "superintendent." The title "executive director" is primarily a title of the social services.

Increasingly, institutional Boards seek financial support and other assistance from corporations; consequently, some Boards have replaced "Executive Director" and "Assistant Executive Director" with corporate terminology, such as "President" and "Vice President," titles which are understood in the corporate world. Thus, when the head of an institution sits down with the head of a corporation, identical titles put the two on an equal footing, which may not be true if one is a "President" and the other is an "Executive Director."

Chapter 4

BOARD/STAFF RELATIONSHIPS

THE RELATIONSHIP among Board, executive director, and staff is a complex and special one. These are three parts of a whole, arranged administratively in a hierarchy, but wholly interdependent with one another.

Responsibility for the total agency belongs to the Board; responsibility for the well-being of children in care and their relationship with their families belongs to the staff. The executive director is in the middle; he is at once the employee of the Board and the enabler for the Board; he is the hirer, supervisor, and administrator of the staff, and simultaneously he is the beneficiary of staff work.

The Board sets policies within which staff must function and establishes working conditions within which staff must operate; the executive director develops and implements procedures which will fulfill Board policies. Administratively, the staff is subject to the will of the executive director and, only through him, to the Board.

Every employee is, to some degree, at the mercy of his employer. Working conditions, salaries, and benefits are rightfully determined by the employer, and the employee agrees to accept those conditions when hired.

The staff of a children's institution is in a somewhat more vulnerable position than most employees, however, because of the uniqueness of the task. A gulf almost inevitably exists between policy makers (the Board) and the staff, especially the child care worker, the person who lives and works most intensively with the children in care. The Board sees the children briefly, periodically, usually when they are on their best behavior. Child care workers live with the kids and help them wrestle daily with their problems. The child care worker is the primary change agent in the lives of residents.

Not only child care workers, but all staff of a children's institution are involved with children. Anyone who receives a paycheck from a children's institution is by that fact involved in child care.

The importance of Board/executive director/staff relationships cannot be appreciated without understanding to some extent the nature of the task.

THE TASK

It is likely that anyone who has not lived with troubled children can understand only partially the intellectual, physical, and emotional energy which are required to work hour after hour and day after day with children who today are appropriately referred for institutional care.

These are children who have not had the security of stable, loving families; who may never have experienced success in anything they attempted; their earlier lives were marked by neglect, abandonment, or abuse—physical, sexual, or emotional; their protest against life may have taken the form of delinquent behavior. Many have had no experience in orderly living, no role model for problem-solving, mature thinking and behavior, no example of deferred gratification. With low self esteem, many of them perceive life as one long, unceasing battle, as did their parents before them.

These children have been separated from their families, more often than not by court order; they may be street wise but academically uneducated; typically they are from one to five years behind in school, and they are not particularly desirous of becoming educated.

When they arrive they may have little sense of direction and less idea that they ever can be successful in anything; they may be impulsive and unpredictable even to themselves; to others their actions may appear totally bizarre. They may be prone to spontaneous aggression or, conversely, they may be withdrawn and silent; they may have periodic fights or make threats, verbal or physical, to adults or other residents.

Child care workers have not just one such child, they have from six to twelve or more such children to work with simultaneously. In addition to working with individual children, child care workers work with the distinctive group these specific children constitute. Group balance and functioning are affected by the disturbance of an individual child and by every new admission to or discharge from the group. The skilled child care worker can harness group influence to quiet an upset child, prevent a runaway or suicide, and to encourage growth of individuals within the group.

Child care workers get up early, they get to bed late, and frequently their nights are interrupted by the needs of a child. Child care workers must be constantly vigilant with respect to any nocturnal activity, which may be simply homesickness, loneliness, or hunger; it may also be a suicide attempt, a runaway, or an alcohol or drug party.

Some Boards—and some executive directors—fail to realize that child care work today is an increasingly skilled position; that the person who lives with the child should be most able to work with him; that "therapy," in terms of a one-hour-per-week interview with the social worker/psychiatrist/psychologist has in large measure given way to the life-space interview.

Under the old pattern, which has been termed the "medical model," a child in residence was expected to talk about his problems only with the social worker, with whom he had a weekly appointment. Any problems which arose in the cottage, on the campus, or in school were referred to the social worker for handling. The social worker was trained to handle problems and was charged with that responsibility. In extreme cases, the child care worker was forbidden even to talk with the child about his problems.

The effect of this model was that the child care worker who lived with the child became primarily a custodian and a facilitator of cottage life, one who made sure that laundry was clean, food served, and that children were faithful to whatever schedule was prepared for them.

One unfortunate, unintended result of this model was that if a child who had a Wednesday appointment with the social worker had a crisis on Monday, the child care worker was the one who had to live with the child for three days until the social worker could address the problem. Often enough, by appointment time the situation had taken care of itself by a runaway, a temper outburst, delinquent act, or other aggression, any one of which warranted a special appointment with the social worker and some of which resulted in summary discharge. Children in crisis are not necessarily easy to live with.

Under the philosophy of the life-space interview, an incident in the life of a child is handled when and where it happens by whatever staff member happens to be on the scene. Every incident or crisis is handled without delay. Rather than providing a living situation which includes an hour or two of therapy a week, today's professional institution provides an environment in which all aspects of institutional life play a part in therapy. This is called a "therapeutic milieu."

In this therapeutic milieu, getting-up time, bedtime, mealtime, playtime, work assignments, interaction with other children and with adults, school, the earning of privileges, learning how to handle anger or other feelings constructively, learning problem-solving techniques, and all other aspects of daily life contribute to the "therapy" of the resident. The intensive hour of "therapy" still may be given in selected cases for definable reasons, but in most agencies it is no longer the primary modality of behavioral change.

These are the children child-care staff work with. Most Board members would not want to change places with a child care worker, and for good reason.

While the needs of the child are being met, the child's family must also be dealt with. When the family comes to visit their child in the institution, they want to talk with the person who lives with their child, not with the social worker, supervisor, or executive director.

As with children, parents are not always easy to get along with. Some are burdened by guilt that the court removed the child from their care and, as a result, they may be depressed or anxious or angry. Frequently they challenge the institution or mock it or demean it; they may be abusive or seductive or manipulative; they may attack the child care worker verbally or physically; overtly or covertly they may encourage their child to break the rules, and they may help him to do so; they may bring drugs on campus and give them to their own child and to his friends; or they may indulge in other inappropriate and objectionable behavior.

Whatever their feelings and whatever their actions, the child care worker must perceive the underlying pain of the parents and react professionally, not personally. Thus, another dimension is added to the child care worker's responsibility: interacting meaningfully with the parents of a child in care.

Obviously, the life-space approach makes substantial demands upon the child care worker, who has become the primary change agent in the life of the child. Counseling, teaching the hazards of unprovoked—or provoked—aggression, modeling mature, responsible behavior; knowing when to console and when to cajole, when it is needful to move into a situation and when it is advisable to back off; teaching problem-solving and recreational skills, helping with school work; distinguishing between the rights of the child, the rights of other children, and the rights of the staff; handling feelings and the behaviors which proceed from those feelings; interacting with parents; using the strengths of the group to manage the cottage and to facilitate maturation of individuals within the group, mediating disputes, and, above all, helping a child to increase his self-esteem are expectations of today's child care worker. Custodianship, laundry, meals, and schedule are mechanical and inconsequential details by comparison.

Children in care, whose lives have been fragmented and unpredictable, must have an environment of consistency and predictability if they are to develop whole personalities. The transition from a disorderly, disorganized life style to an orderly, planful life cannot be made if institutional life replicates the unpredictability of their former life.

Children must receive consistent handling by the child care worker, the campus teacher, the cook, the janitor, the farmer, the work supervisor, the program director, or any other staff member with whom they come in contact. Thus, adequate training for all staff and the development of a team approach among staff are crucial.

Children are quick to sense dissension among staff, and they are skilled at exploiting it. They have an unerring sense of when a staff member is really interested in a child and when a staff member is dissatisfied or is simply holding down a job; they know when a staff member is troubled and preoccupied with his own affairs and when he is free to attend to the children. In one sense, this is a saving grace for staff, for most children are endlessly forgiving of the staff member who makes even major blunders, provided his interest in and concern for kids is genuine. The child is equally unforgiving, and he is merciless toward the staff member who, without concern or commitment, just goes through the motions of providing child care.

Only if staff are free to concentrate on their work can the mission of the agency be fulfilled. Thus, it is imperative the staff be assured that the Board and administration are concerned with eliminating friction and petty annoyances, providing the best possible working conditions, and taking the best interests of staff to heart.

THE CHILD CARE WORKER

Despite the centrality of the child care worker position in the program, child care workers typically do not enjoy high prestige. In most agencies a college degree is not required to become a child care worker, whereas supervisors and executive directors have college degrees and may belong to a particular profession, such as social work or psychology. Training of child care workers is largely dependent upon the employing agency; training requirements by state minimum licensing standards may be as few as 15 hours per year; in most states certification of child care workers is optional, if offered at all; centuries-long tradition, in which anyone who needed a job could become a child care worker dies hard.

In many institutions, child-care staff work on a live-in basis, so that the day does not end at five o'clock as in most jobs.

The usual work week, five days on and two off, is too much for the child-care worker; the work shift is too long; the recuperation period is too short.

Many child care workers know that they are paid less than other employees, who do not live with the children. In a live-in situation, the child care worker remains on duty when other staff leave at 5:00 p.m.; after 5:00 p.m., emergency help may or may not be available on campus. The cottage remains open on weekends and holidays, and cottage staff remains on duty when office staff take a holiday.

Most agencies have just enough child care workers; if one child care worker is late to work or is sick, someone else has to work overtime, which may mean compensatory time or overtime pay, but overtime pay is often at the basic rate, not at time-and-one-half. If compensatory time is given, then someone else has to work overtime.

Typically, the child care worker gets two weeks' vacation a year, supervisors get three, and executives get four. In some work schedules, the child care worker gets additional time off during the year which balances out this inequity; in other work schedules the inequity remains, to the acute awareness of the child care workers.

Under the responsibilities, challenges, and stresses of the child care worker position, petty annoyances become more than petty. The child care worker does not need to be burdened with concerns about job security, increases in salary, arbitrary or capricious policies for which no rationale is discernible or given, or other factors which distract him from his work. He does not need uncertainty about whether or not someone is looking after his best interests; whether someone understands his job and is attempting to improve his working conditions and resources.

Anything the Board and executive director can do to enhance the prestige of the child care workers, to make them feel better about themselves and about what they are doing, to help them feel secure and valued, results in better service to children. Relatively simple things are important. When one Board took the whole staff to dinner, an experienced child care worker commented in amazement, "This is the first time that anyone around here ever bothered to invite me to anything!" Certainly the children in her cottage were handled with greater enthusiasm for at least a few days.

Some agencies have a "Child Care Worker of the Month" or "Child Care Worker of the Year" award; others provide bonuses at Christmastime or at the end of the year; child care workers can be featured in the agency newsletter; news items in the local newspaper can be helpful. Even a Board member's simple "Thank you for what you are doing; we appreciate it" can have meaning to a child care worker, and the comment costs nothing.

Generally speaking, child care workers are not demanding, but they must be assured that they will be heard, that the Board will attempt really to understand the nature of the job and will seek to improve the lot of all employees, insofar as it has power and resources to do so. This is basically reasonable.

DEPENDENCY OF RESIDENTS AND STAFF

One of the limitations of institutional life is that it teaches dependency. The lights always go on, there is always food on the table and gas in the tank; all other necessities appear without any bills being in evidence. Children do not know that Board members and executives work hard to make sure that these things happen. Unfortunately, children assume that this will happen not only in the institution, but that somehow it will magically continue after they leave the institution. This is no one's fault, it's just the way things are. The program should contain specific elements to counteract this natural feeling on the part of residents.

What is often overlooked, however, is that the same thing happens to staff who live on campus. This, too, is no one's fault; it is just the way the system and human nature work.

Salaries in many agencies preclude maintenance by a child care worker of an off-duty apartment or house which can be used only two or three days a week. Some child care workers go camping on all off-duty time because they have nowhere else to go; others visit relatives when off duty. Either of these arrangements bespeaks inadequate salaries and benefits and reinforces the second-class status of the child care worker position.

The executive director, too, is not exempt from creeping dependency. His home may be provided on campus; his lawn is mowed for him, maintenance on the house is performed by the maintenance crew, utilities are free; he may be authorized to draw food from the agency pantry. Subtly, unconsciously, he, too, tends to become dependent.

Staff with lower salaries than that of the executive director are even more vulnerable to this phenomenon. Meals are provided for them, of course, when they are on duty. In many cases, where off-duty housing is provided on campus, meals are still furnished for them when they are off duty. They do not have to go grocery shopping, they do not have to pay rent, utilities are free, they do not have to worry about leaky faucets or broken windows or any of the other minor annoyances of home ownership. They tend to forget about the regularity of normal household bills.

Subtly, insidiously, without being aware of it, they are pushed back to the dependency of childhood, and unconsciously they may arrive at the point where they expect to be taken care of and have decreasing capability of or interest in taking care of themselves.

To offset the effect of inadequate salaries, some agencies provide off-duty quarters for workers on campus. This is a well-intentioned but short-sighted attempt to provide adequately for staff. No employee can fully escape the institutional atmosphere or feeling of responsibility, nor can he get complete rest while remaining on campus. Physical separation from the job and the job location is essential. Every employee should have a life apart from the institution.

Other agencies provide off-campus housing or an off-duty allowance which is collectible at the time the worker leaves campus for off-duty time. These are preferred arrangements.

Best of all, of course, is a salary which is adequate to maintain off-duty, off-campus living arrangements and a work schedule which permits their use.

The Board is well advised to consider carefully the nature of benefits provided for staff. If off-duty, on-campus housing is provided, it is wise to increase the salary and charge rent. Similarly, if off-duty meals are provided, a standard charge for meals for each member of the family and for family guests can be made. Neither staff member nor resident should be protected from the reality of monthly bills.

Institutional life is artificial to some degree for both residents and staff. The Board has a responsibility to reduce that artificiality as much as possible.

Salaries should be adequate for staff to live like people in other positions live.

Some agencies have opted for increasing salaries substantially instead of providing benefits. In such cases, care must be taken that salaries are indeed adequate for staff members to provide for their own medical insurance and retirement over and above social security.

STAFF AS INDIVIDUALS

Success in institutional programming depends upon each staff member's carrying his responsibility and carrying it in harmony with every other staff member.

We have said that the staff is at the mercy of the Board and the executive director. Functionally, however, the Board and the executive director are also at the mercy of the staff. If the staff elect not to function, or, almost worse, to function marginally or at a slightly lower level, the Board and executive director are helpless; the mission of the agency must fail.

Staff members can say one thing in the front office, in training sessions, and in supervisory conferences, but do something quite different when back on the living unit or out on campus working with children. No supervisor can watch a staff member all the time and, even if that were possible, in such a case the worker would not be needed, the supervisor could do the work to begin with.

It must be remembered that child care workers and other staff are not only employees, they are also people, with hopes, dreams, aspirations, fears, and personal goals in life. While their personal life circumstances or needs cannot be allowed to intrude upon their work, their personal goals also cannot be ignored. Staff must be accorded the dignity of any individual.

Like almost everyone, staff members of a children's institution work in order to make a living. Some seek a position in a children's institution because of an inherent concern for children; some because they want to be of service to others; others because the children's institution is the only employer within easy driving distance; and still others because that is the only job available.

Staff are under some compulsion to accept less than ideal working conditions in order to keep a paycheck coming in. The fact that they stay on does not mean they like the working conditions.

If the Board has any intention of providing an adequate program of child care, the cares and concerns of the staff must be accommodated. Staff must be free from personal worries on the job in order to concentrate upon the task at hand. Staff who are not free from concerns about their own self interest are not free to help children to grow.

Higher salaries is a starting point. Other opportunities should also be available to them: the opportunity for promotion within the agency; the opportunity for furthering their education, perhaps with financial help from the agency; broadening the base of their assigned task, such as visiting in the homes of residents, serving as teacher of parenting skills when parents visit; gaining new expertise in the use of group dynamics; and the list is endless. Above all, they need recognition that they are providing a needed service; they need to be heard, and their own goals and aspirations must be validated.

It is imperative that Board, executive director, and staff maintain a relationship which is cordial and professional, which takes the needs and contribution of each into account. Only in this way can children and their families be appropriately served.

THE BOARD AND THE EXECUTIVE DIRECTOR

The Board should be very clear that the executive director is their only employee; they are responsible for him, and he is responsible to them. All other employees are employees of the executive director.

Board members interact and conduct business with the executive director. Other than normal social interaction, the Board does not interact or conduct business with the employees of the executive director, with exceptions which will be noted presently. Employees of the executive director interact and conduct business with him.

Interaction between the Board and the executive director is basically confidential, a matter between employer and employee. The Board and the executive work to establish long-range goals for the agency and to develop the resources by which those goals can be attained. Staff under the executive director are involved in administration and direct care, and they need not be concerned with the struggles of the Board and executive director in the larger picture.

All Board members must be sufficiently professional and attuned to the nature of Board work as not to reveal Board/executive director interactions to employees who are subordinate to the executive director. Even, perhaps especially, if a Board member and an employee are personal friends, a distinction must be maintained between personal relationships and business relationships. With practice, it is possible to divest oneself of personal relationships when the Board sits down to work. The focus is upon the business at hand, in which personal friendships have no place.

This is an important issue. Among other things, rumors run rampant on a campus. The more staff members are tied to the campus, as in having off-duty quarters on campus, the narrower their vision tends to be, and the more susceptible they are to rumors. Given rumors and half facts, their imagination takes over, and they believe the worst.

The executive director should be allowed to give information to the staff according to his own schedule. It is not acceptable for a Board member to pre-empt this prerogative.

THE BOARD AND THE STAFF

Dealings with staff under the executive director are administrative matters; the Board cannot properly direct, hire, or fire employees under the executive director. Any dissension which develops between a staff member and the executive director is an administrative matter and must be settled between the employee and the executive director without interference by the Board. Not all decisions by the executive director can be popular with all employees, but the executive director is hired, in part, to make decisions whether or not they are popular.

If an employee approaches a Board member on matters of agency or personal business, the Board member may listen, but then, without fail, will refer that employee to his supervisor, to the executive director, and/or to the written grievance procedure by which a communication from a staff member is guaranteed to get to the Board promptly.

If Board members have a concern about a particular staff member or a staff member's job performance, they can, of course, share their concerns with the executive director. If the issue is sufficiently substantive and negative, and the executive director takes no action, the Board's option is to deal with the executive director; they do not have the option of interfering with his administration.

This is a crucial point, for staff members will occasionally attempt to bypass the executive director and approach Board members directly, usually with personal complaints. The Board has no business dealing with personal complaints of staff members who are responsible to the executive director unless and until those complaints are filed as a formal grievance.

It is not unknown for Board members, also, to bypass the executive director to deal directly with employees. This is a serious violation of principle on at least two counts: (1) it undercuts the executive director, and (2) it involves the Board in administration.

The rights of the employee are safeguarded by a written grievance procedure which assures the employee of ultimate consideration by the Board if dissension with the administration cannot be resolved by a supervisor or by the executive director. In the absence of a written grievance, the Board has no authority to intervene in administrative matters.

In essence, the Board/executive director/staff relationship resembles an hourglass. The Board is in the top, the staff is in the bottom, and the executive director is in the middle. Communication goes from the Board to the staff through the executive director; communication goes from the staff to the Board through the executive director. In other words, the executive represents the Board and the staff to each other. This principle cannot be stated too often or too strongly. Many boards, executive directors, staff, and agencies have gotten into trouble by not adhering to this principle.

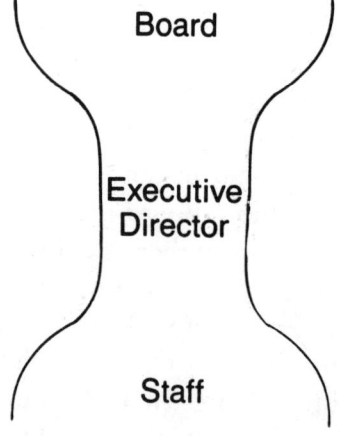

There is one usual exception to this principle: In order to save the time and energy of the executive director and to ensure that the Board members receive a variety of perspectives from within the agency, the Board may request that individual staff members meet with Board committees. This can be either on an ongoing basis or on an *adhoc* basis. That is, the Board may request the executive director to appoint a staff representative to, for example, the Program Committee. This employee may be appointed to this responsibility on an ongoing basis or for a specified period, such as one year.

On the other hand, the Board may request that a different staff member meet with the Board each time the committee meets. A combination of these procedures may be used, also, with two staff representatives, one continuous staff position on the committee and another staff position which rotates among different staff members; for example, the program director meets regularly with the Program Committee; child care workers take turns meeting with the committee.

One other factor must be taken into account. Surface appearances among staff may be deceiving to the Board. What appears to be tranquillity and peace may, in fact, be an armed truce between executive director and staff. More than one executive director has intimidated staff members into silence.

The Board must maintain its vigilance by remaining alert to any clues to subterranean tension or dissatisfaction on the part of staff. Clues may be excessive turnover of staff, the departure of a valuable or high-ranking employee or an employee of long standing, guardedness in conversation by a staff member, constant turmoil in the program, persistent unrest among residents, a high rate of runaways or expulsion of residents, constant program changes, body language of staff, or other factors which the alert Board member will recognize.

Long-term, experienced employees may have insights which would be helpful to the Board but which cannot be made into a grievance because of the risk of discharge.

Identifying such a situation is a delicate issue, for the Board is not to be involved in administration. One approach is for the Board to circulate an evaluation questionnaire to staff as part of the executive director's evaluation. This questionnaire deals only with those parts of the executive director's job description which impinge directly upon staff. A checklist or rating procedure facilitates and focuses responses, and space can be provided for additonal comments. The questionnaire should be returned directly to the Board in a stamped, addressed envelope which the evaluation committee provides. Needless to say, such evaluations are confidential. The concerns listed by staff will be considered in completing the executive director's evaluation, but care will be taken that identity of the source is not revealed.

Care must also be taken in such evaluations that routine, frivolous, superficial, self-serving, or idiosyncratic complaints are not given undue credence.

Another approach is for the Personnel Committee, in its constant effort to upgrade working conditions, to interview individual staff members with respect to overall job satisfaction and working conditions. The Personnel Committee will arrange with the executive director to interview staff. The content of these interviews is also confidential.

If the Board finds substantial dissatisfaction among staff about working conditions, the performance of the executive director, or anything else which affects job performance, a more extensive inquiry should be made.

As a matter of courtesy, whenever a Board member is on campus, he will inform the executive director of his arrival, the purpose of his visit, and he will inform the office when he is leaving. It is unacceptable for a Board member to interact with staff members who are subordinate to the executive director or to prowl around the campus without the executive director's knowledge.

One additional note about Board and the campus. Some Board members wish to be actively involved with children in care. Some wish to take children home for a weekend, to take them fishing or shopping, or in other ways to participate in the lives of children. This is a professional decision which can be made only by the administration.

In the days when most children in care were orphans or were relatively stable children who basically needed a place to live, personal relationships with Board members might have been acceptable. Almost without exception, however, children in care today have families of their own; they are disturbed and problem-ridden, they have few interpersonal skills, and frequently they have a great deal of anger. To expect them to establish a relationship with strangers may be an unreasonable expectation and quite beyond their capacity.

The administration must be free to allow or disallow personal interaction between Board members and children in accordance with the need of the child without pressure or negative comment by the Board.

Such permission requires the professional judgment and the weighing of the dynamics of an individual child, which is the responsibility of the executive director.

Some agencies provide visiting homes for children who have little or no contact with their own families, in order to provide them with some experience in family living. A Board member may qualify for such service, but he should expect to go through essentially the same study process as a family which is unrelated in any way to the institution. Like all applicants, the Board member should be prepared for a turndown on his application. Board membership carries no special privileges with respect to children in care or for violating professional standards. Pressure upon the administration for exceptional treatment of Board members is not acceptable.

The administration must be free to administer the program according to the best professional insights available.

SUMMARY

The relationship among Board, executive director, and staff is crucial to the operation of the agency. The effect of morale upon the program can hardly be exaggerated. Morale will increase in direct proportion to the extent that staff feel they are being dealt with honorably by the Board and by the administration.

If lines of authority and responsibility are kept clear, if the integrity of the functions of the Board and the executive director is maintained, and if the staff perceive that they are being dealt with fairly, staff will be free to concentrate upon the task at hand, and children and their families are likely to be well served.

Chapter 5

COMMITTEES

FUNCTION OF COMMITTEES

THE HEART of the work of the Board is its committee structure and functioning. This cannot be stated too frequently or too strongly. A Board cannot function effectively as a committee of the whole; Board work must be parceled out to committees, which can meet as often as necessary to do their work.

The Board has two types of committees: standing and *adhoc*. Standing committees provide continuity for the basic work of the organization, such as program, plant, personnel, and finance; *adhoc* committees provide for special, usually time-limited functions, e.g., planning a particular fund-raising event, planning a recognition dinner for retiring employees or Board members, etc.

Standing committees are created by Board by-laws. *Adhoc* committees may be established by Board action or by appointment by the Board president, with the consent of the Board, or in some other manner provided in the by-laws.

By amending the by-laws, the Board may create whatever standing committees it wishes to; however, the status of standing committee should be reserved for those functions which will be, indeed, a permanent necessity in the Board's work. *Adhoc* committees cease to exist when their task has been fulfilled; standing committees rarely disappear, even when they are totally inactive or when their function is no longer needed. Generally speaking, the fewer standing committees, the better. The most common additional standing committee is a committee on financial development.

An executive committee, usually composed of the Board officers and committee chairpersons, functions on behalf of the Board between

Board meetings and performs other tasks assigned by the Board. For those few boards which meet monthly, the executive committee may have few occasions to function on behalf of the entire Board.

In general, for a Board that meets quarterly, committees should meet at least four times a year, that is, once in advance of every Board meeting. Some committees will need to meet more often, especially if a special project, such as a building program or a special financial campaign, is underway. Part of the agreement in becoming a Board member is attendance at whatever committee meetings are necessary to conduct the work of the Board.

The special value of a committee is that it can take time to consider fully a discrete assignment and to do the background work which will enable it to bring to the Board reasoned and documented recommendations.

Committees must schedule ample time apart from Board-meeting day to do their work thoroughly. Responsible committee work cannot be discharged effectively in a one-hour meeting held just in advance of a Board meeting, nor can it be done by the Board serving as a committee of the whole.

For example, the Personnel Committee has responsibility for personnel policies. In considering a specific issue, the Personnel Committee will review present personnel policies; it may wish to interview individual staff members, secure personnel policies from other agencies, confer with personnel experts from a university or from industry, secure information from the Child Welfare League of America or the National Association of Homes for Children, and draw on the training and experience of committee members. A committee member who is trained and experienced in personnel matters will be invaluable in speeding this process.

As a result of this research, the committee has ample information on which to base a recommendation which will be appropriate for the agency and which will conform to professional standards. The committee distills its information into a recommendation to be sent to full Board.

Some issues will pass through several committees before being taken to Board, e.g., a request for the establishment of a new staff position would go from the Program Committee (which establishes the need for the position) to the Personnel Committee (which provides a job description and rate of pay) and then to the Finance Committee (which ascertains whether or not the position is within the budget); a request for a new vehicle would go from Buildings, Grounds, and Equipment Committee to the Finance Committee, etc.

Committee recommendations should be sent to Board members in advance of the Board meeting through whatever channel the Board prescribes—through the Executive Committee or directly to individual Board members. Board members must have an opportunity to study the issues which are to be presented for discussion and action, to get their questions in mind, and to relate the recommendations to the work of other committees and to the work of the agency as a whole. Questions in the Board meeting can readily be answered by the committee which has done its homework. With proper committee work, the Board meeting should proceed expeditiously and effectively.

COMMITTEE RESPONSIBILITY

The responsibilities of each committee must be spelled out carefully and completely so that committee members know what is expected of them.

As with all aspects of agency work, committees should set goals for their work.

Committees should keep notes with respect to their work so that their work and the rationale behind the work are on record for future reference and so that committee assignments can be updated periodically.

Committees must be proactive, rather than reactive. The initiative for discharging committee responsibilities lies with the committee chairperson. Neither the president of the Board nor the executive director should be expected to remind committees of their responsibilities.

COMMITTEE ASSIGNMENTS

The Board of the average agency needs at least five standing committees: Buildings, Grounds, and Equipment; Budget and Finance; Personnel; Program; and Nominating. If finances are a problem, the Board may establish a standing Development Committee. Most other work can be handled by *adhoc* committees.

The assignment of each committee must be specified in writing, and committee work is eased if the Board provides instructions by which the committee work should be accomplished.

BUILDINGS, GROUNDS, AND EQUIPMENT COMMITTEE

This committee has oversight of all physical property and equipment. The responsibility of this committee includes, but is not limited to, the following:

1. Makes at least an annual inspection of all buildings and equipment
2. Makes recommendations and presents a budget for maintenance, renovation, elimination, or replacement of existing buildings and equipment
3. Develops an ongoing preventive maintenance program in conjunction with the executive director
4. Recommends acquisition of new equipment, complete with comparative estimates of the cost
5. Maintains a current inventory of physical property
6. Ensures that the physical property is in clean and safe condition for use
7. Recommends a budget figure which will accumulate to replace vehicles or other expensive equipment at specified intervals

Instructions to the Buildings, Grounds, and Equipment Committee might go something like the following, and instructions to other committees should be equally detailed:

- Inspect all buildings and equipment no less frequently than annually
- In conjunction with the executive director, develop a program of preventive maintenance
- In conjunction with the executive director, recommend to the Board a schedule for property renovation, repair, or replacement
- In conjunction with the executive director, develop an annual budget figure for periodic replacement of equipment such as typewriters, vehicles, appliances, etc.
- Receive requests from the executive director for new or additional equipment, and make recommendations to the Board
- Ensure that an inventory of property is maintained on a current basis
- Recommend to the Board acquisition or disposition of property
- Prepare an annual list of needs to maintain or augment physical assets and submit a cost recommendation to the Finance Committee in time for consideration for the next succeeding annual budget

- Advise the Board with respect to any and all leases of property, mineral rights, or other assets and execute the Board's instructions
- Implement the Board's instructions with respect to leasing property, mineral rights, or any use of the agency property
- Act with respect to any aspect of physical property as assigned by the Board or the Board president
- Oversee the farm operation(if the agency has a farm)

It is to be expected that the Buildings, Grounds, and Equipment Committee will make at least an annual inspection of the physical property of the agency. This means virtually a square-foot-by-square-foot, hands-on inspection of all physical property by all committee members. Simply asking the executive director what is needed is inadequate; committee members must have first-hand knowledge of property and equipment. The Board is responsible for physical assets of the agency.

This committee will keep blueprints of all construction in a safe and accessible place.

One item that is frequently overlooked is the underground network of pipes and wiring. The committee should ensure that a map of underground pipes and wiring is made. A frequent situation is for a maintenance man of long standing to carry this information in his head. When he leaves or dies, no one else knows where either pipes or wiring are to be located, which is a real inconvenience and, in case of emergency, can be costly.

Property is the Board's responsibility. The executive director will keep the committee informed about the property from his point of view, but he should not have to remind the Board or a Board Committee of its responsibilities.

PERSONNEL COMMITTEE

The purpose of this committee is to make recommendations to the Board regarding job descriptions, evaluation procedures, employee relations, working conditions, and other related matters. Specific responsibilities include, but are not limited to, the following:

1. Produces a personnel policy manual including, but not limited to, work expectations, vacations, sick leave, time off, grievance procedures, employee benefits, etc.
2. Seeks to upgrade pay, benefits, and working conditions for staff

3. Recommends a salary scale for all employees
4. Approves and recommends to the Board the establishment, modification, or elimination of staff positions
5. Approves job descriptions for proposed positions
6. Recommends or approves evaluation procedures for all staff
8. Reviews applications for the position of executive director; interviews candidates and makes recommendations to the Board for filling that position; develops a contract for the executive director
9. Establishes and implements an annual evaluation of the executive director

Personnel policies are both a guide and a protection for the executive director and for the staff. They provide equitable treatment for staff, and they establish the limits within which the executive director has latitude.

For example, assume that the Personnel Policies provide for one day per month of sick leave. An employee of long standing has an extended illness which has exhausted sick leave and accumulated vacation time. The executive director has no alternative but to terminate the employee or, if Personnel Policies permit, to place him on upaid leave. The executive director cannot exceed Board policies.

The executive director can, however, take the situation to the Personnel Committee for counsel and action. If, in the judgment and upon recommendation of the executive director, the situation warrants extra sick leave, the Personnel Committee can recommend this to the Board. Additional sick leave may be in the form of an one-time grant of additional leave with pay; it may be in the form of borrowing on future accrual of sick leave by the employee, or it may take whatever other form the Board decrees. The Board can exceed its own policies.

Thus, the executive director is protected by the policies from pressure by an employee or resentment by other employees. This situation draws clearly the distinction between policy and administration.

PROGRAM COMMITTEE

The Program Committee plays a key role in the agency. Its specific responsibilities include, but are not limited to, the following:

1. Reviews agency programs with the executive director and/or program director

2. Sends to the Finance Committee a request for the expenditure of funds when program changes are recommended
3. Maintains awareness of program activities
4. Relates program costs to activities
5. Makes recommendations concerning the expansion or curtailment of programs, noting changing costs
6. Promotes training programs for staff. Recommends to the Board specific education or training programs available to the staff on a local, regional, or national basis. Explores the possibility of sponsorship of special training programs for staff within the agency.
7. Provides for evaluation and research with respect to the efficiency and effectiveness of program components
8. Provides program reports to the Board
9. Provides for the periodic use of outside consultants to evaluate the program
10. Familiarizes itself with major concepts in the field of residential care
11. Keeps the Board informed of legislative issues at the local, state, or national level which may influence the operation of the agency; makes recommendations to the Board as to whether such legislation should be opposed or supported; develops and executes a plan by which the Board as a whole or individual Board members, as appropriate, may take action with respect to the proposed legislation

An informed Program Committee makes a dual contribution to the Board. First, it is able to ask pertinent questions of the executive director when a program change or addition is suggested. This is a safeguard for the Board, which otherwise may be tempted to follow the executive director's recommendations blindly.

Second, the Program Committee can serve as a support for the executive director when he makes a recommendation which the Board as a whole may resist or may not understand. An informed Program Committee knows both the Board and the professional issues at stake, thus it is in a better position than the executive director to secure approval by the Board.

Each Board should have members who are experienced in professional child care, and the Program Committee is the appropriate committee assignment for them. The Board is well advised to have at least two persons so qualified, for at least two reasons: first, responsible child care can be offered in a variety of forms and with a variety of methodologies, and the Board should have the benefit of contrasting viewpoints; secondly, a single child care professional on the Board is in a very lonely position. Education of the Board in professional principles and acting to ensure professional performance by the Board and the administration ought not to devolve upon one person.

Program

The Program Committee can use a type of checklist for assessing the quality of the program. The following are the kinds of issues which should be included:

1. Can the administration describe the program briefly and with reasonable specificity? If the administration uses a "canned" program, that is, a methodology of behavioral change which is conceived as a whole, e.g., Behavior Modification, Teaching-Parent, Transactional Analysis, etc., in what ways has the administration modified the program construct to make it applicable to this specific agency? There are many excellent programs on the market, but each must be fine-tuned to fit the specific staff, agency, and children.

2. Are individual goals set for and with the residents? How are the goals set? Where are they recorded? Do residents know what their goals are? How is progress toward the goals monitored? (When on campus, a Board member might ask individual residents what their goals are.)

3. Does the program include an incentive system by which residents can earn increased privileges and freedom? An incentive system is frequently called a "level system," in which residents earn their way from one level to another by appropriate behavior and achievement. Each higher level has increased responsibilities and increased privileges. Does the levels system require enough time on each level for new learning to be assimilated? A program which allows a resident to go up three levels and down two levels in three days probably needs revision.

What procedures exist for monitoring a resident's progress through the incentive system? How frequently and by what means does a resident know how his progress is perceived by the staff?

If no incentive system is used, what mechanism or procedure exists to demonstrate and document that residents are making progress and that they are more mature and more responsible when they leave than when they arrived?

4. What decisions can residents make for themselves?

5. Do residents know what circumstances have to change in order for them to leave?

6. To what degree can residents participate in community activities, e.g., hold jobs in the community, date, attend church, use community recreational facilities, etc.?

7. What control do the residents have over money they have earned?

8. What disciplinary measures are used by the administration? Are disciplinary measures aimed at growth and maturation or at control? Has corporal punishment been banned in the program? If not, why not?

9. Is the average length of stay in the institution less than 18 months? Is the average length of stay calculated statistically, or is it an estimate by the administration? If children routinely are in residence for more than 18 months, what professional reasons are there for this?

10. What policies exist for preplacement visits and placement? Is a preplacement visit required? If not, why not?

11. In what ways does the program prepare older adolescents for independent living? The following are examples of what an adolescent should know or be able to do; such things should be incorporated into a program of preparation for independent living, for which excellent curricula are available:

(a) Know the difference between a checking account and a savings account
(b) Balance a checkbook
(c) Complete an application blank accurately
(d) Follow a recipe
(e) Find a number in the yellow pages
(f) Read and understand job advertisements
(g) Interpret advertisements for apartments for rent
(h) Read a road map
(i) Understand directions on a prescription medicine bottle

12. In what ways does the program involve the families of children in care? Are families encouraged to participate in campus activities, eat in the cottage with their child, or contribute to campus life and activities as they are able? When the child visits home, is the hour at which he is to be returned to campus realistic? Some institutions require a child to return by 5:00 p.m. Sunday from a weekend visit. Unless there is a reasonable rationale for such a requirement, the 5:00 p.m. hour is unrealistic and arbitrary, and it serves mostly to demonstrate the power

the institution has over the parents. This may be more for the convenience of the staff than for the good of the child or his family.

13. What training for child care workers is provided—orientation and beginning training for new workers; ongoing training for experienced workers? Children appropriately referred for institutional care and their families have more complex sets of problems today than a few years ago, and demands upon the staff are proportionately greater. No agency can hire trained child care workers; it must train its own staff. The training program must exceed minimum standards, which may require as few as 15 hours of training per year. Two hours of staff training per week is minimum.

Are all staff involved in training? Every staff member who has contact with children in residence, e.g., cooks, farmer, maintenance personnel, secretaries, etc. should have training so that residents receive consistent handling by all staff.

14. In what ways are the principles of permanency planning implemented?

15. What statistical data are kept by the administration? Can the administration provide precise data as to the average age of residents at admission, average length of stay, average length of stay of child care workers, etc.?

As the Program Committee members become acquainted with the program and with professional child care concepts, many more questions will occur to them.

The purpose of the Program Committee is not to dictate to the administration what the program should be, but to ensure that progressive, professional principles of child care are at work in the institution.

BUDGET AND FINANCE COMMITTEE

The Board *must* retain control of the budget. Only in this way can the Board be assured that the agency assets are being used in accordance with the Board's intentions and that bills will be paid.

The Finance Committee is the Board's major control over the agency, and thus it is one of the most powerful committees. The Finance Committee must give attention to all financial details of agency operation.

Usually the Board Treasurer serves as chairperson of the Finance Committee. Finance committee membership appropriately includes businesspersons who are accustomed to reading balance sheets and keeping income and expenditures in balance, bankers, accountants, investment brokers, etc.

The responsibilities of this committee include, but are not limited to, the following:

1. Prepares an annual budget
2. Reviews and approves accounting procedures to ensure adequate accountability of all agency assets
3. Approves the allocation of funds, payment of bills, and the preparation of financial reports
4. Reviews monthly reports on income and expenditures
5. Reviews and explains deviations from the budget to the Board
6. Reviews and approves budgets of committees and special projects
7. Reviews on an annual basis the sources of funding for the agency in conjunction with preparation of the budget
8. Alerts the Board to an approaching deficit or other financial crisis
9. Arranges for an annual audit of the financial operations of the organization and reports results of the audit to the Board
10. Recommends to the Board the investment or disposition of funds and reports to the Board on a regular basis the status of such investments
11. Reports to the Board other financial matters as deemed appropriate by the Board

All requests for expenditures should go through the Finance Committee. The Finance Committee should require the executive director and every committee which anticipates a new, major expenditure to submit comparative bids. The Finance Committee should also make sure that comparative pricing is used for lesser purchases.

The work of this committee is expedited by charging one committee member with the responsibility of reviewing monthly the general ledger to ensure that expenditures are in accordance with the budget, that all bills have been paid, and that money was expended only for its intended purpose.

One note of caution: fiscal responsibility requires that a monthly comparison be made of expenditures, budget, *and income*. Comparison of expenditures only with the budget is useless and misleading in a deficit situation. Only when income is equal to or greater than the budget is a budget/expenditure comparison meaningful.

If the agency has a sizeable endowment, the Board may wish to appoint a small, special investment committee which is empowered to act quickly with respect to invested funds in order to take advantage of a changing market. Alternatively, one Board member who is experienced in investments may be appointed to manage the funds. For most agencies, the most effective procedure is to empower a commercial investment firm to manage the agency portfolio. The investment market will not wait for Board meetings, or even for a conference call among Board members.

Developing the Budget

The Finance Committee has responsibility for developing the budget and for keeping it under control. Budget control is achieved by meticulous preparation of the budget and constant surveillance of expenditures and income.

Budget preparation is a year-long activity. During the year, a list is kept of additional staff, new equipment, program changes, pay raises, or other new expenditures which should be included in the next fiscal year's budget.

Formal preparation of the budget begins well in advance of the date on which the budget is to be approved. Estimates by committees of projected expenses must be developed with as much factual basis (e.g., competitive bids and comparative pricing), as possible.

Many Boards meet quarterly. Assume that the new budget for a July 1-June 30 fiscal year is to be approved at the April Board meeting. Budget preparation might go something like the following:

1. November. Each committee meets to finalize its plans for the following fiscal year and to develop the cost of those plans. The executive director prepares his budget requests. The Finance Committee meets to estimate income. Plans and cost estimates of the committees and of the executive director are sent to the Finance Committee.

2. January. The Finance Committee meets to consider the recommendations of the several committees and of the executive director. The Finance Committee prepares a budget which shows anticipated income and proposed expenditures. (Alternatively, the executive director, as an *exofficio* member of each committee, may be directed to draft a budget proposal which incorporates committees requests, with supporting documentation.) The proposed budget is sent to the Committees and to the Executive Committee.

3. February. The Executive Committee considers the proposed budget and approves or modifies it and schedules it for consideration at the April Board meeting. If the Executive Committee disapproves the budget, it is returned to the Finance Committee with instructions for revision. The proposed budget as approved by the Executive Committee is mailed to all members of the Board.

Some Boards do not involve the Executive Committee in the budget process. In such a case, the proposed budget is sent by the Finance Committee directly to individual Board members.

4. April. The budget is accepted or revised and approved.

Board members must have the proposed budget in hand in advance of the Board meeting at which the budget is to be approved so they have time to examine it in detail.

Once the budget has been approved, it is the virtually inviolate limit of agency operations, and the Board has the responsibility to ensure that this is so. No requests for expenditures outside the approved budget should be entertained during the budget year except in bona fide emergency. Tornado damage rates as an emergency; a leaking campus water tower is an emergency. Pay raises, the addition of new staff positions, purchase of a vehicle, renovation of buildings (unless a roof falls in) do not rate as emergencies. An emergency is something that could not have been anticipated at budget-preparation time but requires action which cannot be delayed.

The budget process is designed to provide a planful approach to and control of agency expenditures. Barring an emergency, the only appropriate time to request expenditures is in the budget-making process.

The Finance Committee serves as a guardian of the budget. Throughout the year the Finance Committee remains alert to any expenditures which are in excess of budget; it disapproves any non-emergency expenditures which were not included in the budget; it makes a monthly comparison of income and expenditures and alerts the Board when expenditures threaten to exceed income.

The Financial Report

The Finance Committee must devise a financial reporting form which can be readily understood by Board members who are not accountants.

One convenient reporting form lists the budget's line items (salaries, electricity, printing, gasoline, etc.), followed by four columns. The first column contains the monthly budget for each line item (one-twelfth of the annual budget figure for that item); the second contains expenditures for the month; the third column contains the cumulative budget figure for the year to date; the fourth contains cumulative expenditures for the year to date. Thus, every Board member can see at a glance what expenditures were within or were in excess of the budget for the month; the cumulative columns show the status of each line item for the year to date. The cumulative columns are important because some expenditures are seasonal in nature, and although one month's budget may be exceeded, the cumulative expenditures are within the budget.

At the bottom of the form, figures should show clearly whether the total expenditures are within budget or over budget.

The Finance Committee is well advised to develop this form with care. A misplaced set of parentheses or some format which is clear to an accountant may be misleading to some Board members. The form should be sufficiently clear that no calculations are necessary to understand it.

NOMINATING COMMITTEE

The Nominating Committee should be a standing committee, because its work extends throughout the year. By-laws of some agencies authorize the President of the Board to appoint the Nominating Committee; others designate Nominating Committee members by virtue of their office of the Board, e.g., 1st Vice President is Chairperson, and specified committee chairpersons are members; or some other method establishing the Nominating Committee may be used.

Selecting new Board members is much like hiring a new staff member: the Board must know as much as possible about the candidate, the candidate must know as much as possible about the agency, about the Board, and about expectations of Board members.

Identification of candidates for Board membership must be done with care. Too often, just prior to the Board meeting when new members are to be elected, the Board members search their minds for names of people who might be willing to serve, and, as election day approaches, desperation grows to find someone to fill the Board slots.

First, the Nominating Committee, with the help of the Board, should identify the talents or skills required for Board work. Then it should actively seek persons who possess the requisite talents and skills.

The Nominating Committee should devise a personnel form which the prospective candidate will be asked to complete for review by all

Board members. This will serve to acquaint Board members with the candidate's personal and professional background, prior experience as a volunteer and/or Board member, and reasons for interest in the agency.

The invitation to consider Board membership should be made in a personal interview, rather than by telephone. The Board member who extends the invitation can interpret the work of the agency more effectively in person than by telephone, more time is available for the candidate to ask questions, and a personal interview provides an opportunity to respond to verbal and nonverbal reactions to the invitation. Additionally, a personal visit gives more credence to the invitation than a telephone call.

A packet of written material is helpful in introducing the agency to the candidate. The packet should contain at least a brief history of the agency, a description of the need for the services of the agency, a description of program, the current challenges to the agency, and an overall view of the Board, its work, and its expectations.

Before expecting anyone to commit himself to Board membership, it is appropriate that the prospective candidate visit the agency and visit a Board meeting. A visit to the agency gives the prospect an opportunity to see the program in action, to talk with staff members and residents, and to see the property. A visit to a Board meeting helps the prospect decide whether or not Board functioning is such that he will want to join the Board.

The sequence of the Nominating Committee's work, then, is as follows:

1. Identify talents and skills required for Board work
2. Identify candidates who possess the needed skills and talents
3. Secure personal data on candidates
4. Invite prospective candidates to consider Board membership
5. Invite prospective candidates to visit the agency and Board meeting
6. Distribute personnel forms of prospective candidates to Board members
7. Place the names in nomination

The Nominating Committee may appropriately be assigned the responsibility for developing an orientation program for new Board members.

It is not to be expected that every Board position will be filled by persons with different skills or talents. In other words, with a Board of thirty-six members, there may not be thirty-six discrete skills which are needed. The remaining positions may be filled by persons of broad general experience, common sense, integrity, and an interest in the agency and its work. Prior experience on a volunteer board may be helpful.

It should be noted that some Boards ask persons who are not members of the Board to serve on committees. This arrangement is most effective for a limited time and for a specific purpose, as when special expertise is needed temporarily. If the contribution of a particular person is required over a long period, the more satisfactory arrangement is to invite that individual to become a Board member so that he can have voting privileges.

EXECUTIVE COMMITTEE

The primary function of the Executive Committee is to act for the Board in matters that cannot be deferred until the next Board meeting and to carry out specific assignments made by the Board.

The Executive Committee should never be permitted to function as the Board or in place of the Board; it functions only on behalf of the Board. The distinction is crucial.

All actions of the Executive Committee should be ratified by the next succeeding Board meeting and recorded in Board minutes. Board members are equally responsible for Board actions; therefore, every Board member has a right to vote on every issue, even retroactively. If the Executive Committee is empowered to act without Board approval or subsequent ratification, every Board member who is not on the Executive Committee has been deprived of his voting privilege and therefore is held accountable for someone else's action.

Decision-making authority should not be given to the Executive Committee except under emergency or other unusual circumstances, and then only under closely circumscribed conditions. If it is found that the Executive Committee frequently makes decisions for the Board, the organization of the Board and the ordering of its work should be reexamined.

Certain decisions should never be delegated to, or permitted by, the Executive Committee. The Executive Committee cannot make a decision to change the mission statement, to purchase or to sell property, to hire or fire an executive director, or to make a change in agency program, target clientele, or funding.

Empowering the Executive Committee to act on its own leads to an erosion of Board authority and tends to concentrate the power of the Board in the Executive Committee. This is an abdication of Board responsibility which is to be avoided. If the Executive Committee can wield the full power of the Board, the rest of the Board is superfluous.

Emergency Decisions

The most common use of the Executive Committee is to act in an emergency which cannot wait for a full Board meeting. The following are examples:

The central heating system breaks down in mid winter; repair costs exceed the executive director's limit to authorize. He reports by telephone to the chairman of the Buildings, Grounds, and Equipment Committee, who makes a conference call to committee members. Upon recommendation of committee members, the chairman arranges with the Board President to hold a conference call of Executive Committee members. The Executive Committee authorizes the repairs and reports its action to the next Board meeting for ratification.

The executive director reports to the Buildings, Grounds, and Equipment Committee that the agency tractor broke down in the middle of haying season, and a new tractor must be purchased immediately. The Committee chairperson makes a conference call to committee members, who instruct the executive to rent a tractor or to hire someone to get in the rest of the hay. Tractors rarely break down irreparably, and further investigation is required before making a major purchase. In any event, a major purchase like a tractor is beyond the authority of the Executive Committee.

The annual sanitation inspection reveals defects in the agency kitchen which will not pass inspection. Repairs exceed the executive director's limit to authorize.

The executive director reports by telephone to the chairman of the Buildings, Grounds, and Equipment Committee. The chairman contacts the sanitation inspector to get a first-hand report and to identify alternative plans of action. An emergency meeting of the committee is preferable; a conference call may suffice. The chairman reports to the Board president, who calls a meeting of the Executive Committee or, through a conference call, authorizes the necessary expenditure.

A resident drowns in a boating accident. The executive director informs the Board president, who informs the Executive Committee members by telephone. A memo is sent immediately to each Board member for informational purposes, knowing that any Board member may be queried by a reporter or by other interested persons.

It should be noted in these examples that the committees function even in an emergency. The committee chairman does not arrogate unto himself the authority of the whole committee, even when available courses of action appear to be limited.

Assignment of Details

The Executive Committee may be charged with details of Board operation, e.g., reviewing a proposed budget, preparing the agenda for a Board meeting, following up on a Board decision to ensure implementation, representing the Board in meeting with an outside consultant, making a presentation to the United Way, etc.

The Executive Committee may be asked to review the budget proposed by the Finance Committee and include it on the Board meeting agenda or make suggestions for revision.

The Executive Committee may be directed to prepare the agenda for the Board meeting. The agenda should identify the issues to be considered and should be distributed to Board members prior to the Board meeting. Board members are expected to give thought to the business to be considered at the Board meeting before the Board convenes.

The Executive Committee requests committee chairmen to submit committee recommendations or other agenda items by a specified date for distribution to Board members in advance of the meeting. The Executive Committee checks past Board minutes for old business which must be considered.

One appropriate assignment for the Executive Committee is the maintenance of official archives.

Archives start with an official record of Board and committee actions. The Executive Committee may direct the Board Secretary to keep a complete file of Board and committee minutes, correspondence, names of Board members, by-laws, etc. At the end of the official Board year, these documents should be put in a binder, labeled for the year, and stored at the agency. The official record should be other than the Board notebook the Secretary uses during the year, for that is a personal document and contains the Secretary's notes and miscellaneous scribblings.

In addition to written documents, an official file of pictures should be kept. Whenever a change is made on campus, e.g., a new building constructed, an old building removed, a new parking lot installed, a road changed, a new sign erected, etc., a picture should be taken and entered into the archives. If pictures of children in care are included, they should be labeled with the children's names.

Tracing the history of the development of an institution is frustrating without adequate records. Institutions should change over the years, and the means for reviewing agency development should be preserved.

The Executive Committee may also be charged with determining that permanent records are kept of all children who have been in care. A simple form is appropriate, which gives pertinent data including at least, but not limited to, the name and home address of the child, identifying information on the family, and dates of admission and discharge of the child. Periodically, institutions receive requests for verification of birth dates and residence to substantiate applications for social security, and those records must be available.

Keeping the full case record forever is not practical, nor is it necessary. The Executive Committee may set a time limit, such as five years, for retention of full case records, after which the permanent form will be completed and the bulky record destroyed.

Implementing a Board Decision

With respect to ensuring implementation of a Board decision, assume that the Board has authorized a maximum expenditure of $10,000 for an office computer. The Board as a whole has little interest in the precise make or model of computer; its concern is that whatever computer is purchased be adequate for the task at hand and be the best buy.

The Executive Committee is directed to work with the Executive Director to make this purchase. A Board member who is knowledgeable about computers or who has contacts among computer dealers may be asked to work with the Executive Committee. A Board member may know someone who is not a Board member who could serve as consultant in this purchase, and the Executive Committee may invite him to assist in the process.

The executive director is instructed to outline the tasks for the computer and to secure comparative bids. As with all agency purchases, good stewardship of funds must be exercised. The cheapest computer is probably not a good buy; the most expensive probably is overkill.

The Executive committee examines the tasks for the computer as outlined by the executive director, checks the specifications which have been developed, and reviews the bids. When the Executive Committee is satisfied that the best machine for the purpose has been identified at the best price, it authorizes the purchase and then reports the purchase to the Board. If the purchase can be made for less money than authorized by the Board, all the better; the money saved can put to good use elsewhere. The fact that the Board has authorized a given amount does not mean that it must all be spent.

Use of Consultants

The Board should use an outside consultant periodically to make an objective assessment of agency operations. For this purpose the consultant is hired by the Board, not by the administration, and the consultant's report will be made to the Board.

The Executive Committee may be directed to work with the consultant to establish the purpose of the consultation and to convey the Board's intentions. Depending upon the nature of the consultation assignment, the consultant may need to talk with some or all Board members, which usually will be done on an individual basis rather than in a Board meeting. In other cases, the consultant may obtain from the Executive Committee any information that is needed from the Board.

In either case, the consultant makes his report to the full Board, rather than to the Executive Committee. The report should be made in writing. After Board members have had an opportunity to study the report, the consultant meets with the full Board to answer questions or for discussion. The Board will instruct the Executive Director to cooperate fully with the consultant.

The administration will want to use consultation periodically in program development, in which case the consultant works for the Executive Director, not for the Board. This consultant may wish to meet with the Board or representatives of the Board, in which case the Executive Committee would be the appropriate representative group. The report of this consultation will be made to the executive director.

Representation to United Way

An agency which receives funds from the United Way must make an annual presentation to justify United Way funding requests. This presentation is the responsibility of the Board, not of the administration. This task may be assigned to the Executive Committee, which will work closely with the Executive Director to prepare the presentation. The presentation should be made by a Board member, usually the president.

Thus, representing the Board and acting temporarily on behalf on the Board are legitimate functions of the Executive Committee; making decisions for the Board, except on a temporary, emergency basis, is not a legitimate function. When emergency decisions have to be made by the Executive Committee, those decisions should be ratified by the full Board at the earliest opportunity.

DEVELOPMENT COMMITTEE

If income is a problem for the agency, appointing a standing committee on financial development is appropriate. A Development Committee has the responsibility to increase income. The committee should include members who have fund-raising experience in other settings.

The Development Committee works closely with the executive director to plan the fund-raising activity. The Committee should not expect the executive director to carry out the committee's plans, however. Responsibility for fund-raising belongs to the Board.

If the agency has a director of development, the committee works jointly with both the executive director and the director of development to develop fund-raising plans. The director of development is the staff person to implement the decisions of the committee as those plans are approved by the Board.

The director of development should be accountable to the executive director, not to the Board. As the executive director is responsible for administration of the program, so must he have authority for interpretation of the program. If nothing else, he must have veto power over ideas of the director of development.

In the absence of a director of development, the executive director can assume such public relations responsibilities as personal appearances to interpret the program and the gathering of information for a newsletter. Acknowledgment of gifts can be routinized under the executive director's guidance, provided adequate secretarial staff is available. Shortcuts can be used, which will be noted presently.

The executive director cannot reasonably be expected to carry all of the responsibilities of a director of development.

Endowment

The most satisfactory long-range solution to financial probems is a permanent endowment. An endowment is invested; only the interest on the endowment is used for operations. The endowment should be sacrosanct. Donors expect their endowment gifts to endure, not to be spent for operating purposes. The Board is well advised to frame the endowment in such a way that the principle cannot be touched, no matter how desperate the financial crisis becomes. The Board's responsibility is to make sure that a financial crisis does not arise, so that there is no temptation to tap the endowment fund for operations.

Building an endowment is a slow process. As awareness of and interest in the agency grows among supporting constituents, the agency may be included in wills. These will bring in substantial funds some years hence, but of course, bequests are not a quick answer to bill-paying.

A memorial gift program has been helpful in building an endowment in many agencies. A memorial gift program provides a mechanism for interested persons who wish to honor or memorialize loved ones or mark special occasions and simultaneously to support a program in which the donor is interested or which has been of interest to the person being honored or memorialized.

A memorial fund provides that a financial gift may be made to the agency in lieu of giving flowers at the time of a death. This gift becomes a living memorial, which expresses love in perpetuity through service.

Birthdays, anniversaries, retirements, or other special occasions can be honored by similar gifts. One lady requested her friends to make a contribution to a particular agency in lieu of giving her birthday presents. Knowing that the agency was financially poor, she arranged with the executive director to use any such gifts to provide desserts for the children in care.

Education of the supporting constituency is necessary so that persons interested in the agency will think of gifts to the agency when they wish to honor or memorialize someone.

Memorial brochures have been placed in funeral homes, where they may suggest a memorial gift at a strategic moment. Some agencies have been careful to keep lawyers informed of the availability of the memorial gift program or the need for bequests, knowing that many persons look to the lawyer for suggestions when making out wills.

Other agencies provide for family endowments. For an initial gift of a set amount, usually at least $1000, a family endowment is established which can be added to at any time by any member of the family for any reason whatever. A family endowment can be designated for a particular purpose, such as education, off-campus care, medical needs, etc. The donor has a right to designate his gift for whatever purpose interests him. With some education of constituents, a family endowment might be established to pay the light bill, fuel bill, or to take care of other expenses which are intangible and less appealing to some donors.

Every agency periodically receives a sizeable donation, anything from $2500 on up. The temptation is to spend it immediately on needed bills or repairs. Unless the agency is really in dire financial straits, the Board should consider carefully whether such a windfall ought not be added to the endowment so that it will produce income in perpetuity.

The Board must decide which gifts go into the endowment fund and which go into the operating fund, the building fund, or to some other fund. This is a Board decision, not an administrative decision.

Needless to say, all such gifts must be acknowledged promptly by the agency, both to the donor and to the person being honored or to the family of the person being memorialized. Careful records must be kept with respect to all gifts. The Board should ensure that current and accurate, permanent records are maintained and that acknowledgments are timely and accurate. A routine procedure must be established for speedy processing and acknowledgment of these gifts.

Endowment funds are invested to ensure that the highest yield consistent with safety is achieved. Management of the portfolio must be entrusted to someone who is experienced in investment management and who has the time and will take the time necessary to manage the portfolio effectively. This latter phrase is crucial: a volunteer fund manager or a Board-member manager may be willing, but he may not have the time to manage the portfolio properly. A professional fund manager is preferable; management costs can easily be recovered by income generated by effective management.

The Board should consider reinvesting a portion of the interest income. Certainly an amount equal to the annual inflation rate should be reinvested so that the endowment does not shrink. Some Boards routinely reinvest an additional proportion of income, such as 10 percent, so that the endowment continues to grow even if no additions are made to the endowment during the year.

Sponsorship Program

For many years, agencies have operated sponsorship programs. Traditionally, the sponsor has received a picture of the child and in some cases expects to receive letters from the child. Unless carefully planned, however, a sponsorship program causes more problems than it solves.

First of all, there is a problem of confidentiality for the child. Few children need to have their picture and full name sent to strangers.

Secondly, the nature of the problems of children in institutional care today generally precludes their interacting meaningfully with strangers. Typically, today's institutional child has difficulty in interpersonal relationships, and expecting him to respond to someone he has never seen and may never see is futile. Residents have enough problems of their own; they need no help from the agency in finding new problems.

In the third place, institutional care is increasingly short-term—less than two years—and both agency and sponsor must contend with a constantly changing assignment of child to sponsor.

Finally, this type of sponsorship tends to teach dependence and manipulation to residents, a version of what has been called "learned helplessness." Children in care are masters at manipulation, and they know very well how to pull the heartstrings of sponsors to get for free things they could—and should—earn.

An anonymous sponsorship program is acceptable. Donors can be informed that $53.00 will support a child for one day; $35.00 will provide food for one child for one week; $240.00 will provide clothes for one child per year (or whatever the actual figures are), etc. In this manner, donors can relate their gift to the actual service provided without compromising a particular child.

Some groups are willing to underwrite the food bill or electric bill for one month, or to purchase a new vehicle or other piece of equipment. Relating a dollar amount to a specific purchase is meaningful to many donors.

Public Relations

Educating supporting constituents is a continuing challenge. They need to know what the agency is doing and why continued contributions are necessary and how they are used. The best interpretation of the agency's program is a personal appearance by a staff member, who can tell about the program, give anecdotes about children in residence, and answer questions.

Slide presentations have long been used for this purpose, either by a speaker from the agency or without a speaker but with a script. The slide presentation with a script can be sent to remotely located groups when a speaker from the agency cannot appear. The script and the slides will give an overview of the agency program and tell the agency story. The script is carefully marked to show when slides need to be advanced.

Video cassettes are excellent for public relations, because the program can be seen in action; children can be seen moving and playing on the campus and going about their work. Video cassettes can be sent to groups or used in conjunction with an oral presentation by an agency representative. A simple video can be made of "A Day in the Life of X Institution," showing children on campus going about their business over the course of a day. Other agencies have professionally-made movies or videos for public relations purposes, which are also excellent, but these tend to be expensive.

If the agency cannot afford to have a film made professionally, a member of the Board or one of the supporting constituents may be skilled with a video cassette and be willing at minimum cost to make a film which is quite suitable.

Board members should represent the agency in these public relations efforts. They may solicit the help of the Program Committee and executive director in anticipating questions which will be asked and in formulating appropriate responses.

Most state minimum licensing standards forbid the exploitation of residents for public relations or fund-raising purposes, which is appropriate. It is unfair to identify any child as being in need or to parade him before the general public as a recipient of services. No child should be expected to give his personal history in public or be expected to express in public appreciation for the agency and what it has done for him.

Some agencies have a choir or other performing group which tours for public relations purposes. This is a marginal practice; its acceptability depends upon the nature of the presentation which accompanies the concert. Care must be taken to avoid exploitation of residents.

Whenever the picture of a child appears in a slide series, a video tape, a news release, or in an agency brochure, or when a resident participates in a choir concert or other performance for public relations, a release signed by the parents must be in hand. The release, which stipulates that the child will not be identified, simply gives permission to use the picture of the child or participation of the child in public relations presentations. If this release is made a part of routine intake procedures, when an unexpected opportunity arises for the use of a picture, no one needs to scurry around to find the parents to secure a release. Without a signed parental release form, it is safer not to use the child's picture or to use the child in a public performance.

A word should be said about correspondence. The physical appearance of letters or other documents of the agency is part of public relations. Every letter that goes out from the agency is a representative of the agency. Letters should be neatly typed, properly spaced, and words should be spelled correctly. Sloppily-typed letters, or letters which contain crude erasures or misspelled words convey a negative impression of the entire agency. Self-correcting typewriters, which eliminate the need for erasures, have long been available; word processors and many typewriters today have built-in dictionaries, so there is little excuse for misspellings. The agency secretaries should consider each letter to be a work of art, and the executive director should be sensitive to this area of public relations, which is under his jurisdiction.

Reports or records of the agency should be prepared with equal care. The Board should ensure that proper attention is given to these matters, for they may make a difference in income.

Newsletter

One of the most common vehicles for public relations is a periodic newsletter published by the agency.

As the name suggests, a newsletter contains news, especially about children in care. Pictures are helpful. Many executive directors reserve a section of the newsletter for themselves. A column from the executive director is a good place to educate supporters about the agency program, about child care, about legislative issues, about the needs of families, or other, related topics. A brief item may list specific or special needs of the agency. Most newsletters carry a list of donations, listing the name of the donor and the name of the person being memorialized or honored.

Publication dates of the newsletter should be consistent. A common publication schedule is quarterly. Publication is easier if the newsletter is built into the agency schedule so that the newsletter goes out in the same month each year.

A professionally done newsletter is not cheap, but it is worth the investment. With the advent of personal computers and desktop publishing, the production cost is coming down. Professional consultation in newsletter layout is a good investment, for the newsletter, like correspondence, represents the agency, and it must look good. If the newsletter is sloppy, contains bad writing, has misspellings or poor grammar, or otherwise is put together in a slipshod manner, readers will draw a negative impression about the entire agency. Hiring professional composition for the newsletter is one of the shortcuts which can be made in the absence of a director of development.

Proposals

Proposals can be written to solicit support from foundations or corporations.

A directory of foundations should be standard equipment for every agency. The directory lists the foundations throughout the country, the purpose for which the foundation exists, the size of the average grant, and any geographic restriction on grants.

Foundations vary widely in the kinds of projects they will support. Some foundations are interested only in capital improvements; other foundations will contribute to almost anything except capital improvements.

Some foundations will supply funds for a pilot project of a new program. Others will assist in funding a new staff position, with diminishing support over a period of time; for example, a foundation may provide full funding for a staff position for the first year, half funding for the second year, and one-quarter funding for the third year. By the fourth year the agency is expected to assume full financial responsibility for the position.

Every large corporation devotes funds to charitable purposes for which application can be made. Like foundations, corporations may have specific targets for their charitable contributions; they may have a particular interest in health or education; or they may restrict their charitable gifts to a particular geographic area. The Board member who is employed by a large corporation can advise the agency with respect to charitable funds from his own employer and also with respect to the procedures to be followed in approaching all corporations.

It should be noted that proposal writing is a time-consuming and somewhat technical task which cannot appropriately be assigned to the executive director. The Development Committee (or the Board, in the absence of a Development Committee), may hire someone who is experienced in proposal writing to write the proposal; if the agency has a director of development, this would be part of his duties.

Media

A director of development is expected to develop contacts among the media—radio, TV, newspapers, and magazines—so that newsworthy items from the agency will appear in the media promptly. Any public reports of activities of the agency or on campus are helpful in reminding the public of the existence of the agency.

The director of development or an agency representative should work with radio and television stations to produce Public Service Announcements, which are free.

The executive director does not have time to make these contacts effectively; they depend upon a director of development.

Other Fund-Raising Methods

Some agencies sell life insurance policies with the agency as beneficiary; the premiums may be tax deductible.

Other agencies have special fund-raising events, such as auctions, style shows, raffles, concerts, etc., which usually are used to raise operating or special-purpose funds.

These special events should be organized and conducted by Board members. They have more substantial standing in the community than the executive director, and they can devote more time to special projects than can the executive director.

Many agencies overlook possibilities for increasing income from assets which they already have. Every aspect of the agency operations and possessions must be scrutinized to increase income from assests. Help is available in many areas, e.g., the agency which has a farm can consult with the Farm Bureau, the County Agent, or a university extension to help plan for most effective use of farm land.

Equipment which has outlived its usefulness to the agency can be sold. Property which has been received as a bequest can be sold if this is consistent with the intention of the donor. Unused space or property can be rented out, with due attention being given to tax implications.

Some agencies have developed an investment plan under which constituents invest funds with the agency, receive a set interest rate during their lifetime, and, upon their death, the principle belongs to the agency. Some religious denominations operate foundations which will provide this investment service for member institutions.

Still others seek donors who will contribute on a regular basis, such as monthly or quarterly. Some donors want to be billed for this contribution, simply to be reminded of their pledge. A self-addressed envelope is a small investment for a regular contribution. Donors may reasonably be expected to supply the stamp for the return envelope.

The Board should take into account the fact that supporting constituents have a vast reservoir of talent, much of which may be donated to the agency if the needs are publicized. They cannot offer to meet a need if they do not know a need exists. A note in the newsletter will bring surprising results. One interested supporter may come to the campus to take professional pictures; another may be skilled in film-making or publishing; another may own a car dealership and be able to assist in providing vehicles, etc.

The possibilities for fund-raising and public relations are limited only by the imaginations of Board members and of the professionals whom they employ.

SUMMARY

As said at the beginning of this chapter, adequate committee work is the heart of Board work. From the dimensions of committee responsibilities, it is clear that committees must schedule ample time for their work.

A successful Board will assign Board members to the committee where their skills can be used most effectively, will ensure that each committee has appropriate instructions, and will be guided by the considered recommendations of the committees. Every Board member should be assigned to a committee, but, except for *adhoc* committees of short duration, no Board member should expected to serve on more than one committee at a time.

Chapter 6

THE BOARD MEETING

THE BOARD MEETING is a meeting between the Board and the Board's only employee, the executive director. This is part of the employer/employee construct. Together, the Board and the executive director plan for the agency.

The Board meeting is a place for decision-making. Decisions are based upon information and recommendations of Board committees and of the executive director. Board decisions are not always popular, but they must be made, popular or not. As stated previously, each decision should be related to the mission of the agency.

Some Boards have been slow to adopt business procedures in the work of the agency, which is a residual effect of the orphanage days, when institutional administration was simple enough that Board members could do it. Make no mistake about it, institutional care today is big business. No agency today can afford not to utilize business-like procedures. The Board is accountable for its actions, and whatever techniques from the business world can be used to make that accountability more effective and more efficient must be utilized. Today's agency operates in a highly competitive society, federal funding and state funding are subject to change, and ultimately only the most efficient agencies will survive. Board membership includes diverse skills so that many talents and viewpoints will be available to the Board.

The Board meeting is where of these things come together.

When the Board sits down in a meeting, friendships and personal preferences are put on "hold" until the Board meeting has adjourned. Board members are not in a popularity contest; they must control the agency.

THE SETTING

With rare exception, a full day should be allotted for each Board meeting. Scheduling a Board meeting for 3:00 to 5:00 p.m. on a Sunday afternoon really is not adequate to provide for adequate discussion of issues. Furthermore, scheduling a Board meeting with a firm adjournment time jeopardizes the Board's work.

At least half of the Board meetings should take place on campus. This may be the only time some Board members visit campus after orientation. The Board meeting should discommode campus life as little as possible.

The Board meeting should be held in a room that is separated from a normal flow of traffic and from distractions. Board meeting day on campus is not an appropriate day for lawn fertilizing or mowing, for noisy maintenance within earshot of the Board room, payday for the kids, or a ball game. The Board should be protected from distractions and interruptions.

The room should not be so large that the Board will be lost in one corner of the room, e.g., gymnasiums are generally inappropriate for Board meetings, nor should it be so small as to give a cramped feeling or to limit the flow of air. The room should be large enough so that each Board member has some elbow room and has space to move around without inconveniencing anyone. Accoustics may be a factor in room selection: people should be able to hear and understand each other without strain; a room that echoes is an annoyance.

Each Board member needs a flat surface on which to open the Board notebook and to spread paper which may be passed out in the course of the meeting. This can be either a table or a chair with a writing arm.

Discussion is facilitated among Board members if the seating arrangement permits each Board member to see the face of every other Board member. Arranging chairs in rows, all facing the same direction, promotes discussion between a Board member and the chairman, rather than among Board members, which is counterproductive to Board work. Additionally, those sitting in the back have difficulty in hearing those who are in front.

If the Board is not too large, it may fit around one table. Several tables can be put together to form a solid or hollow square. Chairs with writing arms can be arranged in a circle.

Someone should be assigned the responsibility for the physical arrangements for a Board meeting. Occasionally during the meeting unexpected needs will arise, and the Board needs to know to whom to turn to get that need met. If the Board meets on the campus, the executive director has this responsibility.

Frequently a coffeepot, cups, spoons, sugar, cream, and napkins are available for use while Board members gather and throughout the day. With increasing frequency, a variety of diet and standard soft drinks also is offered.

Whoever is in charge of physical arrangements should be sensitive to the needs of Board members during the meeting: when someone is too warm or too cold; when the sun is in someone's eyes and a blind should be drawn, or when other needs become apparent, action should be taken before a request is needed. The attention of Board members should be on the work at hand, not on physical details of the meeting room or normal supplies or equipment for a meeting.

In advance of the meeting, the person in charge of physical arrangements should ascertain whether a flip chart, chalk board, overhead projector, slide projector, VCR, or other equipment will be required and, if so, should arrange to have it on hand and ready for use. Electrical equipment, such as overhead projector, slide projector, etc., should be plugged in and ready for use, with a screen already set up, if needed, so that the time of the whole Board will not be taken up by searching for an extension cord, finding the electrical outlet, and manipulating machinery or equipment. Appropriate supplies such as chalk and eraser, pens for the flip chart or overhead acetate, etc., should be checked. Extra pencils and writing pads may be provided either at each chair or in a conveniently available place in the room.

If the campus does not have a parking lot, signs on the campus directing Board members where to park are helpful.

The location of bathrooms should be obvious or marked.

The basic principle in preparing the site for the Board meeting is to have a meeting place that is reasonably comfortable and quiet, equipped to meet the needs of the Board, but to impose as little as possible on the agency staff and residents. The business of the staff is kids, not Board members.

BUSINESS

The purpose of the Board meeting is to make decisions. If committees have functioned properly, the work of the Board should proceed expeditiously.

The agenda for the Board meeting, minutes of the previous Board meeting, committee recommendations, and other pertinent information should be mailed to Board members in advance of the meeting. The mailed agenda should include actions to be taken so that Board members have an opportunity to consider the issues before they come to a vote. The Board chairman is reasonable in expecting Board members to be acquainted with this advance information.

The agenda may be organized something like the following:

1. Approve minutes of previous Board meeting.

Reading of the minutes is unnecessary if the minutes have been mailed out ahead of time. Board members are expected to note on their copy any changes or corrections to be made, so changes or corrections can be recorded quickly and the minutes approved.

2. Ratify actions taken by the executive committee since the last Board meeting.

In nearly every case, executive committee action will be sufficiently separated in time from the Board meeting that executive committee minutes can also be mailed to Board members in advance of the Board meeting. This speeds ratification, for Board members have an opportunity to formulate in advance any questions they may have. If executive committee minutes have not been mailed, they must be read for ratification.

3. Old business.

In preparing the agenda for advance mailing, the executive committee or some Board member, usually the Board Secretary, should be directed to review previous Board meeting minutes to extract issues on which closure has not been made. Only by giving conscious attention to past Board minutes can unfinished business be concluded. Too often, uncompleted business is buried in Board minutes and only resurrected five years later when the issue surfaces again or when someone happens to go back through old Board minutes. Constant vigilance is required to keep Board business current.

Frequently, Board business is unfinished because additional data are needed for a Board decision. In this case, the issue is referred to the appropriate committee, and the committee has the responsibility for gathering the necessary data and bringing the issue before the Board at its next meeting. This does not, however, preclude a review of Board minutes in preparing the agenda.

The review of goals belongs to old business. Short-range goals should be reviewed at every Board meeting. Long-range goals should be reviewed at least annually. Long-range goal review will take place more dependably if it is a standard agenda item for one specific Board meeting, e.g., the first or last meeting of the fiscal year, the first meeting after new Board members are seated, the official annual meeting of the corporation, etc.

Committee reports may be presented in two parts, the first part dealing with old business, the second part dealing with new business. If this is to be done, committees should be so informed in advance so that they can organize their reports accordingly.

If committee reports are organized in this manner, old business of the committee is presented at this time.

4. Executive Director's report.

The report of the Executive director is basic to the Board meeting, for it presents the current status of the agency and of the program. Ample time must be provided to hear and to discuss the executive director's report.

It may be anticipated that the executive director's report will review the positives about the agency. The executive director would be less than human if he did not accentuate the positives of his administration. The Board will find it helpful if the executive director provides statistics to support his positive interpretation of agency progress. Not all progress can be presented statistically, however, and the professional judgment of a properly qualified executive director must be given credence. Board members are able to distinguish between bona fide success and reports of success which are primarily self serving.

The agency operates in a complex society, and it is not to be expected that everything about the administration will be positive. The Board should not only expect, it should insist, that the executive director's report include the negatives, or the problems and challenges which the agency faces. Few things are more distressing to a Board than to have a series of positive reports from the executive director and then suddenly to be confronted by a serious situation which has been months or years in developing.

It should be stated that the executive director will be honest and forthright in his report in accordance with the reception given previous negatives by the Board. If the Board has been sympathetic and supportive of administrative problems, the executive director will report with candor. If the Board has not been supportive, the executive director can hardly be blamed for glossing over the negatives. A climate of openness and mutual support must exist.

As part of his report, the executive director may request subordinate staff members to appear to report on various aspects of the program and to respond to questions from Board members about those parts of the program. Especially in a large agency or in an agency with a complex program, the executive director cannot know every detail of the program. Subordinate staff should have a more nearly complete grasp of details of certain aspects of program operation than the executive director, and the Board should have an opportunity for dialogue with responsible staff members in order to obtain the most nearly complete information available.

When the subordinate staff members have made their contribution, they should be excused. The Board meeting is for the Board and the executive director. Only the executive director is responsible to the Board; all other staff are responsible to the executive director.

5. New Business.

If committee reports were organized into old and new business, new business emanating from committees is now presented. If committee reports were not so organized, committee reports appropriately follow the report of the executive director.

Any other new business is offered at this time.

6. Adjournment.

Before the Board adjourns, the next meeting date should be set, or, if meeting dates are decreed by the by-laws, Board members should be reminded of the date and location of the next meeting.

One simple device which expedites Board work is the publishing of an annual calendar. The calendar shows Board meeting dates, the dates committee reports are due, the dates nominations for Board membership are due, and any other dates pertinent to Board work. Brief notes can be made on each Board meeting date: election of Board members, long-range goals review, review of audit, etc. As committee meeting dates are set, they can be added by each Board member. The calendar should fit into the Board notebook so that it is easily accessible.

The effectiveness of the Board meeting depends upon the activity of the committees. By being informed in advance of the issues to be decided, Board members can have their questions ready. If committees have fulfilled their assigned responsibilities, they are prepared to respond to questions without delay. The Board meeting should proceed efficiently and effectively.

The Board meeting is not a place to generate new information; it is a place to act on information which has already been supplied.

BOARD MINUTES

Care must be taken with Board minutes. Board minutes should reflect action taken by the Board; they should also indicate the rationale behind the actions so that the line of thinking of the Board can be recovered at a later date.

The Board Secretary has two options for recording a rationale: he may include the rationale in making a record of motions made and passed, or he can refer to specific committee meeting minutes which contain the background for a particular decision. If he chooses the latter course, the reference should be specific, e.g., "See minutes of Finance Committee, March 3, 1988."

If official archives are maintained (See Chapter 5, Executive Committee, Assignment of Details), the committee minutes to which reference is made will always be available, and subsequent Boards will be able to recapture the thinking behind a decision.

It should be noted that the Board Secretary should take the minutes of the Board meeting. Using a secretary or other staff member from the agency is inappropriate for this purpose. Minute-taking is facilitated by committee reports, which contain specific recommendations to be made and by the agenda which is mailed in advance. Additionally, a tape recorder can be used to record the meeting so that the Secretary has a back-up system.

BOARD LUNCHEON

If the Board meeting is an all-day meeting and lunch is to be served, the lunch should be set up in a room apart from the Board room so that preparations can be made while the Board is at work. If the lunch is served at the Board table, the Board has to quit work, clear away all papers and wait for lunch arrangements to be made. After lunch is over, each Board member has to get reorganized, which wastes time and causes confusion.

A word about the Board luncheon. Frequently, especially when the Board meets on campus a full, sit-down meal is prepared.

Board meetings on campus are necessary; they are also an inconvenience for staff, who typically are admonished to make sure that the grass is freshly cut, the cottages are immaculate, that kids are clean, well dressed, and instructed how to interact politely with Board members, and all staff are expected to use their party manners. The Board should intrude as little as possible on the life of the agency.

Some agencies have special sets of dishes and elegant equipment for the use of the Board only, which has to be hauled out of a remote cupboard, washed before and after use, and stored again after lunch. Agency cooks take pride in bringing out their best recipes for the Board meeting and spend much time and energy preparing for the Board luncheon. This is objectionable on two counts: first, the cooks are hired to feed children, not the Board, and the best recipes should be used for kids; secondly, especially in today's calorie- and weight-conscious society, adults who are in an all-day, sit-down meeting do not need a heavy meal in the middle of the day. Disposable dishes, cups, and cutlery save much time and energy. If food that is good enough for residents is not good enough for Board members, the residents' menu needs revision.

Board business will proceed more expeditiously in the afternoon if the lunch is light. A buffet luncheon is appropriate, with an emphasis on salads or other light foods. The reputation of the cook is not at stake, and simple food can be arranged attractively. If finances permit, the lunch can be catered, which saves extra work for the cooks.

The lunch break is a good time for Board members to walk around the campus and to chat with whatever staff or children happen to be available.

BOARD RETREAT

Scheduled Board meetings usually have full agendas which consume all available time. Typically, a Board has little time in its regular meetings to explore new ideas extensively or to philosophize about the Board, the agency, its program, its clients, and its future.

To provide for a more leisurely discussions, some Boards periodically hold a weekend Board Retreat. All Board members go to a motel, a conference center, or some other location removed from telephones, from the daily schedule, from the need for decision-making, and from the pressure of adjournment time.

In a Retreat, Board members have the luxury of time to generate and explore ideas which elsewhere might appear impractical; they can discuss problems which are not amenable to quick solutions; they can afford to dream, to let their imaginations have full sway. They are free to play "What if.....?" Retreat participants are not under any compulsion to devise solutions; usually retreats are not designed for decison-making. Ideas which initially appear to be wildly fanciful can be entertained and, in the absence of pressure, unexpectedly workable ideas may emerge.

As with all meetings, a successful Board Retreat depends upon preparation. A Retreat which is entirely free-wheeling may be less productive than one which is given initial direction. Some format or plan is needed, but planning should allow ample time for consideration of any ideas which pertain to the work of the agency or of the Board.

An overall Retreat theme may be helpful. The Retreat theme may be one specific aspect of the Board's work, or it may be a generalized overview.

A time agenda is needed to provide structure for the Retreat. The agenda should include total-group meetings, small-group meetings, and free time. Any reasonable agenda is acceptable; the challenge is to provide stimulation and an environment in which Board members can escape from their usual thought patterns and look afresh at their work. Retreat time should contain a balance of work and relaxation. Discussions interspersed with play are doubly fruitful.

A consultant may be brought in to address the group about some aspect of the work of the Board or of the agency or simply to be available as a resource. The consultant may give an initial speech, after which the presentation will be discussed in small groups. On the other hand, the initial speech may be purely inspirational or challenging.

The consultant may participate in the discussions of the Retreat and wind up the Retreat with his presentation, summing up what he has heard and putting his professional interpretation on it or relating what he has heard to professional concepts.

Board members may be organized into small groups for discussion purposes. If small-group topics are decided upon in advance, a consultant may be brought in to meet with each small group. The visiting leaders may serve as facilitators of the small groups or they may serve the small groups as a resource.

Instead of consultants, group facilitators who are not Board members may be used to guide the work of small groups. Nonmember facilitators are free to concentrate upon group process and have no vested interest in the discussion.

Small-group meetings may alternate with total-group meetings. Additionally, the ideal Retreat location contains numerous places where conversational groups can gather apart from scheduled meetings. Such areas should be open and in plain sight, for conversational groups will form and re-form spontaneously on a casual basis.

Some record should be kept of total-group and small-group discussions and of the activity of the Retreat as a whole.

If finances permit, a Retreat is a good time to include the spouses of Board members. Spouses are unsung heroes of Boardmanship. They share their spouses with the Board, they take care of the kids, give up the family car, and keep the home fires burning while the spouse attends Board meetings and committee meetings and spends time on other Board activities. Spouses rarely receive any thanks or acknowledgement of their contribution.

Some entertainment for spouses while Board members work is appropriate during the Retreat. If there are places of interest in the area, tours can be arranged, or the conference physical facilities may offer recreational opportunities of interest. Spouses may be invited to join total-group meetings so that they get a better idea of what the Board is all about.

A Retreat is an excellent mechanism for enriching the work of the Board. The relaxed atmosphere of the Retreat tends to produce new ideas, renewed commitment to the task, and an enhanced spirit of cooperation. The Board which has not held a Retreat has a treat in store.

SUMMARY

Effective Board meetings do not happen by accident; they are the result of thoughtful planning. Basic to the Board meeting is committee work which has preceded the Board meeting. The Board cannot function without adequate information, which comes from committees and from the executive director. A logical sequence in the Board meeting agenda is productive. Committee recommendations should be included in the agenda which is mailed to Board members prior to the Board meeting. The executive director's report must be afforded a fair and thoughtful hearing.

Thoughtful attention given to the meeting room, equipment, parking spaces, and lunch break will facilitate the work of the Board.

As was said at the outset, Board membership in a children's institution should be a highly rewarding volunteer activity. A well-planned Board meeting will leave Board members with a feeling of satisfaction and accomplishment.

To augment the regular meetings of the Board, the Board is well advised to consider a periodic Board Retreat to enrich its work.

Part II

PRINCIPLES AND CONCEPTS OF RESIDENTIAL CHILD CARE

MEMBERSHIP on the Board of Directors of a children's institution is one of the most interesting of volunteer activities, for children are endlessly fascinating, and there is a special poignancy about children who have been neglected or abused or who have other needs. It takes more than compassion or good intentions today to do justice to children and their families, however.

Board members are not expected to be experts in services to children and their families. They are more effective Board members, however, if they have an awareness of major concepts in the field of residential care.

Part II contains principles and concepts of residential child care which should be understood by every Board member.

Institutional care today is partly a matter of the heart, as it always has been, but it is increasingly a matter of the head, of expertise, of professional knowledge, procedures, and concepts. "Lady Bountiful," yesteryear's lady of fashion who went among the poor with a basket of goodies on her arm, has no place in today's welfare system. Pity is out, professionalism is in. Emotion is tempered; good business sense and professional competence are the order of the day.

Today's Board member must know in broad strokes the principles and concepts of professional child care. Board members should not worry about the fine details—those belong to the administration. All Board members should take time, however, to understand the foundation of present-day residential child care so that they have a common core of knowledge, a common point of departure in their discussions.

Aside from being more interested in that which one understands, the informed Board member is in a better position than the uninformed

Board member to direct the agency in professional paths. The Board member who knows the basic concepts can ask more cogent questions of the administration and understand more readily the responses. Service on the Board will be more meaningful, and the effectiveness of the Board will be enhanced, by increased knowledge.

The Program Committee and the executive director will help Board members gradually to broaden and deepen their understanding of the work of the agency.

The basic concepts which follow give the Board member a head start in understanding some of the program issues. Answers are provided to questions which are frequently asked by Board members. No pretense is made that these concepts will turn Board members into professionals in the field; rather, the material is intended as a basis for understanding the work of the agency. These concepts may bring into focus agency activities which otherwise would be beyond understanding.

Chapter 7

SUPPLEMENTAL PARENTING

BACKGROUND OF SUPPLEMENTAL PARENTING

WHENEVER one person seeks to help another, the fundamental question is, "Who owns the problem?"

Everyone needs help from time to time; problems are sometimes overwhelming. At that moment what is needed is help, not usurpation. Only the person who owns the problem can solve the problem. Others can identify or provide resources, they can support, encourage, direct, counsel, and guide — but they cannot solve the problem if the problem is to remain solved.

To have someone take over our problem or solve our problem for us is to be diminished, to be returned to a state of childhood dependency when adults made our decisions for us and determined what we were to do and what our life was to be.

Furthermore, when someone solves our problem for us and the solution fails, we are guiltless, we have a scapegoat: we were not at fault, we did not fail — whoever took the problem from us failed. We are therefore free to continue our inadequate ways and, probably, to fail again.

By the same token, if someone takes our problem and solves it, no credit belongs to us. We have not grown, we have not learned, for we have not acted, and the likelihood is that we will make the same mistake again. Too often, would-be helpers mistake a plan — their plan — for a solution. A plan may lead to a solution, but only if it is the plan of whoever owns the problem.

Conversely, to solve our own problem is to be adult, to be mature, to be in command of life instead of being commanded by life. It is in the process of solving problems that we find that problems are not inherently insolvable; in the process of solving one problem we find the capability to work on other problems, finding strength we perhaps did not know we had. It is these strengths, often unrecognized or unsuspected, which can be augmented and set in motion by the help of others. Maturity is not compromised by accepting help.

Throughout the centuries, people who had problems and needed help typically had their problems taken away from them: the unemployed were indentured; the poor were consigned to an almshouse; debtors were cast into prison. This effectively took the problem away from the person whose problem it was and forever hindered him from finding a solution on his own. This was a well-intentioned but misguided effort which did more for the contentment of the helper than for the benefit of the helped.

This general approach was long used for families who could not provide adequately for their children. Children were placed in institutions and then allowed infrequent contact—or no contact at all—with their family. This was the norm. Society considered the parents to be the "bad guys," and social welfare system, including institutions, to be the "good guys," who knew how to handle and rear children.

Children were placed in institutions because, in the judgment of society, the child's parents were neglectful or abusive. Society saw the child's neglectful or abusive family from the perspective of a normal family, however, of an ideal family, of all families, and society judged the child's family accordingly. To replace this neglect or abuse, society provided a substitute "family," either a foster family or an institution. The parents were totally replaced in the life of the child. The foster family or the institution staff substituted for the family. This was substitute parenting.

When one substitutes for, one takes over on behalf of, or takes the place of, as a substitute teacher takes full charge of a class when the regular teacher is absent.

The child, on the other hand, perceives his family as good and normal. He knows only his own family, and he must believe in his family, for his family is his only hope of survival. If other families are different, it is they who are strange. The child derives his sense of identity and sense of worthfulness from his own family, whatever it is. He belongs in his family. As long as his family is around, there is someone to whom he has value.

To the child, no one can substitute for the family. We now know that no one can replace the parent in the mind, life, and emotions of a child. The child can be taken out of the family, but the family cannot be taken out of the child. The family is a permanent part of the child; it remains in his memory, his dreams, his longings, and his fantasies. Nothing is as important to him as returning to his family, even though with them he was badly used.

The object of services to a child and his family is to help them to find ways of living together, not to help them to adjust to life apart from each other. It must be remembered that, barring a court order to the contrary, the child has right of his family; the family has a right to their child.

Some institutions have been diligent in their attempts to keep child and family separated. Visits have been prohibited, incoming mail has been intercepted, filed, and never delivered; outgoing mail has been censored, telephone calls have been eliminated.

The more rigorously someone attempts to keep the child separated from his family, however, the more determined the child may be to get back with his family or to keep contact with them. He may run away, he may misbehave so as to be expelled, he may secretly mail letters when off campus, he may communicate with his family through friends, etc.

In recognition of the irreplaceable nature of the family to the child, supplemental parenting evolved.

Supplemental parenting recognizes that some families are sufficiently troubled that the child cannot *at this time* receive the nurture which is necessary for safety or for reasonable maturation. Something must be added to, or subtracted from, the family in order to supply the climate within which healthy growth and maturation of the child can take place. In some families, the situation is so acute that for reasons of physical or emotional safety the child must be removed while change is taking place.

The intention is not to separate the child and family permanently; the intention is to separate them just long enough for healing of relationships to take place. The goal is not to make the family into an ideal family, but to help it to improve to the point that the child has a reasonable chance for physical and emotional safety and maturation within the family.

Because a family is inadequate in some ways does not mean total inadequacy. Because a child cannot receive adequate nurture from his family one year does not mean that this will always be so. Every family has some strengths, although they may be obscure and hard to find, perhaps covered over by external circumstances which defeat the parents.

The question is how to provide adequate nurture for the child while preserving the child/family relationship which is vital to the child's growth.

PRINCIPLES OF SUPPLEMENTAL PARENTING

In the concept of supplemental parenting, all of the nurture of a child is a teamwork function. The parents are encouraged and assisted to provide as much of the nurture of the child as possible, but when they come to the end of their abilities, others—social worker, foster parent, or institution—take over so that together, as a team, the parents and the helpers can provide total nurture for the child.

The child is not expected or encouraged to forget or denigrate his family; he is helped to experience his family, to retain a sense of the reality that is his family, to hold onto that which is good and to understand and cope with that which is not good in his family life.

Families whose children are placed have widely varying strengths and weaknesses, and they vary in their capacity to provide nurture for their children. Earnest, sensitive, and extensive effort with such families frequently has been found to be effective in motivating and enabling them to increase their involvement with their own child. This involvement cannot take place if the institution or agency takes their problem from them.

One family (Family A below) is so severely disorganized that the parents can invest themselves only to the extent of one or two visits a year plus an occasional postcard. This investment, although meager, is honored, because it helps the child retain a sense of reality of his family and helps him to establish and to preserve his identity.

In this case, the agency provides the major portion of the nurture, supplementing that which the parents can give.

With another family (Family B below), the situation is not so severe; the problem may be fragility of the physical or emotional health of one or both parents or of the marital relationship; the stress of caring for an active or rebellious child on a full-time basis is unbearable and, if continued, will result in the breakdown of the family.

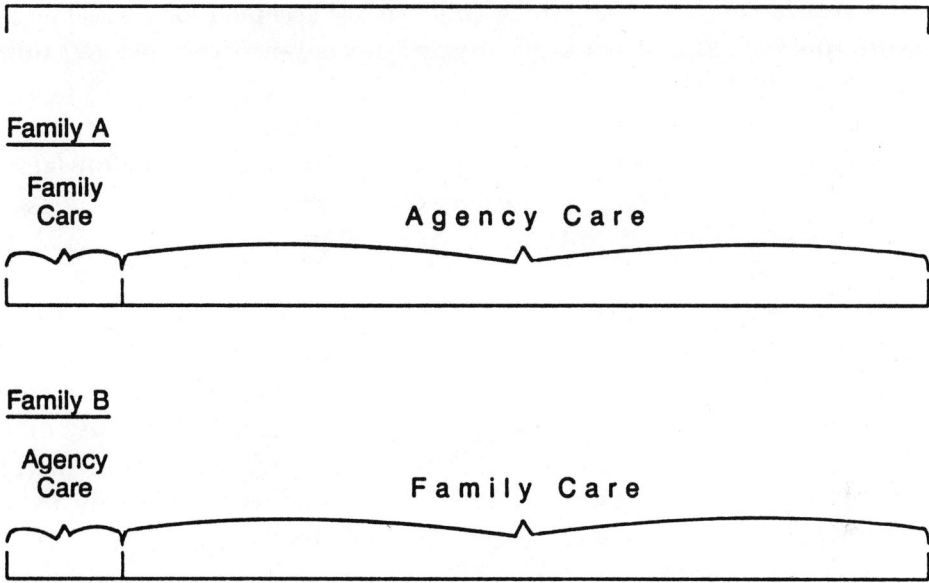

For this child, institutional care may appropriately be a five-day-a-week arrangement, wherein the child lives in the institution and attends school during the week, but spends every weekend at home. The child's primary focus and source of support is his family. In this case, the family provides the major portion of the nurture, and the agency provides relatively little.

Other families are situated at various points along this line. Wherever the family leaves off, the agency begins—but it does not do anything for the child or the family which the family can do for itself.

With particular application to residential care, supplemental parenting means that the parents of a child in placement (or other persons of significance to the child) remain actively involved in the life of the child. They are neither encouraged nor permitted to evade or abdicate their responsibility to the child.

If the social worker who placed the child works with the family of the child in care, the institutional program supplements that work and coordinates its own work with the work of the placing worker and with the growing strengths and capabilities of the family. The Board must assure itself that this is, indeed, happening.

If the social worker who placed the child does not have time to work earnestly with the family of the child in care, the institution must assume that responsibility. This, in turn, may alter the intake policy by limiting the geographic area from which children are accepted for care. The institution staff cannot work effectively with parents who live 250 miles away.

In the best possible scenario, the institution provides service to the family concurrently with providing care for the child. Conjoint family therapy, group meetings of parents of children in care, teaching and modeling of parenting skills, involvement of the parent in the life of the cottage, and other techniques of family strengthening thus become possible on campus.

The child will visit home as frequently as is feasible; the family will visit the child in the institution. The family will take the child clothes shopping, will sign his report cards, attend school functions, or in other ways participate in the child's life as they are able. Some institutions send children's clothes home to be laundered, primarily to remind parents on a weekly basis that they have responsibility for a child. The laundry case is an excellent way for a mother to send treats to her child.

Institution staff send brief notes to the parents reporting an improved school grade, announcing the child's forthcoming participation in a school activity, reporting a week's improved behavior, or any other event in the life of the child which will enhance the image of the child in the minds of the parents. In whatever way is appropriate for a particular family, the parents are kept involved in the life of their child. The methods of parental involvement are limited only by the imagination of the staff.

If there is a secret of success in work with the child and his family, it is that no one will permit the family to abdicate their responsibility for the child, that they will be helped to meet their own needs as well as the needs of the child, and that the child welfare system will provide only that nurture for the child which the family cannot provide.

Without doubt, many families who could have remained involved with their child were not motivated to do so because the social worker simply did not have the time to work with them. This is not a criticism; this is reality. Effective work with multiproblem families is enormously time- and energy-comsuming, and many placing workers simply have too many cases to be able to spend sufficient time with one family to gain their trust and then to help them improve their functioning. This is tragic for the child and for his family.

It must be acknowledged, of course, that some parents are totally unable to carry even partial parenting responsibility, and the likelihood is that they will never be able to do so, or they will not be able to do so within a reasonable period of time. Children get older day by day, and parental adequacy cannot be indefinitely deferred. In such cases, other arrangements must be made in planning for permanent, alternate care for the child. The child may be placed in adoption, or the plan may call for long-term foster care, either of which may become, indeed, substitute care.

Such cases must be viewed with caution, however, lest caregivers make unwarranted assumptions about the parents' interests and abilities. Many parents who are somewhat inadequate are intimidated by professional persons or by offices, and they may simply be too timid or frightened to speak up. Many of them have been through numerous social service agencies, and they feel that they are expected to be inept, lazy, and uncaring, or perhaps preoccupied, obstinate, or just plain uncooperative. With a history of failures and of repeated humiliations and condescensions behind them, it is not to be wondered at that they are hard to motivate.

Fewer persons are totally inadequate than is commonly believed; almost all of them have some strengths, and it is the responsibility of caregivers to uncover those strengths and help the parents utilize them.

The first challenge to the child welfare field is prevention of family disintegration. The second challenge is restoration of a child to his family at the earliest possible moment.

The Board of Directors, through the Program Committee, should require that the agency be involved in work with families, and it should evaluate periodically the agency's effectiveness in this work. If there is any realistic hope that the family will be able to resume care of the child, the agency's work must supplement, not replace, the parents' work.

Chapter 8

PER CAPITA COST AND OCCUPANCY RATE

BOARDS OF DIRECTORS are understandably concerned about the number of children for whom care is provided, the size of cottage groups, the occupancy rate, and the cost of care. The institution exists to serve children, and it would appear that the more children who are served, the more effective the institution is.

PER CAPITA COST

Boards are rightfully concerned about the cost of care, and they know that the greater the number of children, the lower the per capita cost of care, for there are more children among whom to spread the expenses.

The most accurate institutional cost figure is the daily per capita cost, which is what it costs to provide care for one child for one day. In order to compute costs accurately, a record must be kept of the number of child care days provided, i.e., how many days each child was in care. The total number of child care days provided in one year is divided into the total expenses for the year to determine the daily per capita cost.

Assume that the annual expenses totalled $100,000. If 15 children were in care for the full year, 5475 days of child care (15 children x 365 days) were provided; the daily per capita cost is $18.26. With the same expenses, if 10 children were in care for the full year, 3650 days of child care (10 x 365) were provided; the daily per capita cost is $27.40. By extension, the annual cost per child is $6,664.90 and $10,001.00 respectively.

Most states' minimum licensing standards set a maximum cottage capacity for single-staff coverage. That is, no more than a given number of children can be cared for by one staff member. The most expensive child in any cottage is the first child, for the cottage must be as fully staffed for one child as for eight. When the maximum allowable cottage capacity is 8, the second most expensive child is the ninth child, for when this child is accepted for care, cottage staff must be doubled.

The institution and the cottage have certain fixed costs, costs which continue irrespective of the number of children in care. The light and heating bills are virtually unchanged with one or eight children, child care worker salaries are unchanged up to the legal capacity of the cottage, cooks have to prepare food for one child or ten, etc. These costs cannot be changed, but with increased numbers of children, the *per capita* cost is reduced. In this way, the money used to support the institution appears to be used more efficiently by being spread among larger numbers of children.

Supporting constituents (and perhaps the new Board member) will occasionally remark about the high cost of child care in the institution, commenting, "It doesn't cost me that much to raise my children!" Such a comment provides an excellent opportunity for interpretation of institutional expenses.

Part of the contrast between institutional costs and family costs is the fact that parents do not receive salaries, benefits do not have to be paid (social security, unemployment insurance, workman's compensation, retirement), and grass seed, gasoline, the light bill, the mortgage payment, painting and wallpapering, the cost of a new car, and other common household expenses are not considered to be part of child care in a family. In the institution, all of these expenses are included in the cost of child care.

While it is true that the Board must be alert to efficient use of funds, keeping expenditures down, and getting full value for the dollar, it is a fallacy to expect child care to be cheap or to expect to reduce costs simply for the sake of saving money. Good institutional care is expensive.

As with most things, one gets what one pays for. Better job performance can be anticipated from a staff member who is paid in accordance with job requirements. Expectations can be put on a child care worker who is paid $20,000 per year which would be inappropriate for a child care worker who is paid $10,000 per year. Increasingly, specialized services are required on campus: educational evaluations, psychological or psychiatric counselling, specialized educational programs, paid recreational staff, and others, and these all cost money.

An active volunteer program can serve to flesh out the program, but volunteer help is never free: someone on the staff must be charged with the responsibility of recruiting, orienting, assigning, supervising, keeping the roll of volunteers, and assessing the effect of each volunteer's work. Operating a volunteer program without a staff coordinator is an invitation to confusion. Volunteers need to know what is expected of them, with whom they are to work, when, where, for how long, and for what purpose. Staff and residents must know that volunteers will appear on schedule for stated purposes. Lack of a coordinator results in reduced or erratic attendance by volunteers, which results in disappointment or bitterness for staff and residents.

Good child care is not cheap, nor should the Board attempt to make it so.

OCCUPANCY RATE

With the per capita cost of care in mind, some Boards urge the administration to increase cottage capacity and to accept more children into care, which appears to be logical.

The situation is more complicated than it seems.

It must be remembered that the cottage is not a place for children to come just to live. The cottage is a place of healing, learning, unlearning, relearning; it is, as has been stated before, a "therapeutic milieu"; children come for a purpose, they have work to do, and they have goals to work on. They cannot achieve these things alone; staff members are heavily involved with each child individually and with all of the residents collectively, as a group.

In considering the number of children in a cottage, the dynamics of providing care and an opportunity for healing and growth for troubled children must be taken into account. Children who are appropriately accepted into institutional care are troubled children, or they are children from troubled families, usually both. They have problems with self esteem, with interpersonal relationships, with family, with attention span, with school, with work details, and the world in general. They do not always get along with each other.

Some children are hostile, some are aggressive, some are withdrawn, or in other ways they are not necessarily easy to live or deal with; their inner turmoil is evident in the course of cottage life. This is the primary reason for limiting the number of children who can be in the charge of one staff member, who sometimes feels more like a referee than a child care worker.

Despite careful intake procedures, and irrespective of the adequacy of the pre-admission study and procedures, no one can guarantee in advance that a particular child will fit into a specific cottage group. That can be determined only after he arrives and goes through the settling-in process.

Finally, and most importantly, the number and nature of children in a cottage group is only part of the picture. The most significant factor in cottage life is the number of sets of relationships which exist among children in a cottage.

A set of relationships is defined as follows: Person A relates to Person B; Person B relates to Person A.

Person A ——————— Person B = One set of relationships

The number of relationships increases exponentially while the number of children increases arithmetically.

Number of Persons	Number of Sets of Relationships
2	1
3	3
4	6

The formula for calculating these sets of relationships is $x = \frac{y^2 - y}{2}$, with Y representing the number of children in the cottage. With 10 children in the cottage, then, $10^2 = 100$; $100-10 = 90$; $90/2 = 45$. Thus, with 10 children in care, there are 45 sets of relationships. However, these are one-to-one relationships only: A and B relate; A and C relate; B and C relate, and so on.

Groups do not function only on a one-to-one basis. A,B, and C are on the basketball team together; A,B, and E are on the baseball team; B,E, and G are on a debate team; A,E,F, and G are involved in delinquent acts together, B,C,D, and G are all employed at MacDonald's; A,B,C,F,G, and H are involved together in some other activity, etc.

The calculation of possible sets of relationships must take into account every possible combination of two's, three's, four's, fives, sixes, etc. This is a more complicated formula, the result of which is as follows:

Number of Persons	Number of Possible Sets of Relationships
10	1022
11	2046
12	4094
13	8190
14	16382
15	32766

As can be seen, with each additional child the number of possible sets of relationships is approximately doubled. When the group has 20 persons, there are more than one million possible sets of relationships; when the group size gets to 31, there are more than one billion possible sets of relationships.

One of the things children in institutional care tend to have in common is difficulty in interpersonal relationships. To place such a child in a situation where he has 4094 or 8190 or more possibilities for interpersonal relationships is to invite failure for the child. One can perceive quickly the problem of increasing cottage capacity.

Thus, when a Board member hears a child care worker say "I have had ten children instead of eleven for the past month, and it seems so peaceful," the crucial factor is not the fact that there is one less child; the important thing is that the possible sets of relationships have been cut in half.

Experts in group work suggest 8 as an ideal number for a group. With eight members, the group has diversity, but the group is not large enough that subgroups are likely to form. Sub-groups can be positive, but they can also be negative. A negative subgroup is generally known as a "gang."

Another trap that Boards fall into is to become concerned that beds be filled immediately after they are emptied. It is common for numbers of children to be discharged at the end of a school year, at the end of the semester, or at other times of the year. When a number of beds thus become vacant, when a new cottage is opened, or when a cottage which has been closed is reopened, the Board may expect the cottage to be filled immediately. This cannot be done if professional principles of child care are adhered to.

Every group in time develops some sort of balance; some residents become leaders and others become followers. In other words, each group has it own "pecking order." Whenever a child joins the group or leaves the group, the balance of the group is changed. A leader may be superseded, a new leader may emerge, followers may change group roles, etc. A new child must find his place in the pecking order. Will he be a leader? Will he be a follower? Will he become a scapegoat or doormat for the rest of the group?

After one child departs, time must be allowed for the group to adjust before a new child is introduced into the group. If the child who left was particularly popular, the group members must be allowed a period of "mourning." Everyone is sad to some extent when a friend or loved one departs, and everyone deserves time and opportunity to express that sadness. If the new child is brought in before the group "mourning" process is complete, the group may dump onto the new child feelings that have nothing to do with him. "Who does he think he is, taking Johnnie's place, sleeping in Johnnie's bed and using Johnnie's closet?" Group resentment will put an undue and inappropriate burden on the new child, who has his own adjustment to make to a new setting. This is unfair, for the group feelings which are thus being expressed have nothing to do with the new child; he simply happened to be in the way.

Conversely, if the child who left was especially unpopular, the group members must be allowed a time to "celebrate." Again, if a new child is brought into the group before this process is complete, the hostility, anger, or other feelings which really concern the departed resident may devolve on the new child, which is equally unfair. A new child should have to contend only with his own merits or demerits; he should not have to contend with ghosts of former residents whom he didn't even know.

It is reasonable to expect the child care worker to know the status of group life in the cottage, which is distinguished from knowing the individual children in the cottage. The child care worker should be able to say, "The group is not ready for a new admission yet; it has not fully regained its balance from Johnnie's leaving." Or, "The group is not ready for a new admission just now; we are working up to X crisis, and we need to get that out of the way before a new group member is brought in." Or, "Yes, the group is ready for a new admission." Part of the training of child care workers involves training in group work, and the child care worker has the responsibility for learning to make such assessments.

When a group has recovered its balance following the departure of a group member, it is ready to accept a new resident. New group members can be brought in only one at a time, with an interval between admissions. The length of the interval between new admissions depends to some extent upon the degree of disturbance of group members and the degree to which group work is in operation in the cottage; the more disturbed residents are or the more tenuous the group cohesion, the greater the interval must be. As a rule of thumb, a two-week interval is appropriate for a group of relatively healthy children and where the group process is effective, although this varies from group to group or within one group from time to time.

Similarly, if a new cottage is opened or a closed cottage is reopened, the cottage group must be built up gradually. Chaos lurks around the corner for the institution which moves eight children into a cottage simultaneously. Even if children are moved from other cottages into the new cottage, the move must be made with care. These children probably do have the advantage of being acquainted with each other, but they have never had to live together; living in different cottages, they have never had to establish group dynamics with each other.

Other factors are at work with respect to filling empty beds. The philosophy of permanency planning has led to a rethinking of the appropriate uses of institutional care, and fewer children are being referred to institutions than a few years ago.

The relationship between the institution administration and referring agencies and the reputation of the institution for excellence of service bear on the number of referrals. Institutions which have a good track record for providing professional care of children will have sufficient referrals to fill their beds; institutions with lesser programs will have proportionately greater problems in filling beds.

The Board must be guided by the administration with respect with which beds are filled. Staff members who are involved with the children in care on a daily basis are in the best position to determine when a group is ready for a new member.

On the other hand, if referrals persistently are below the institution's capacity, the Board, through the Program Committee, will want to take a fresh look at program quality and the relationship between the institution and referring agencies.

This is the time when it is helpful to have a board member who represents consumers of the agency's services.

The Board is appropriately concerned about the occupancy rate. Before complaining to the executive director about empty beds, however, the Board should be sure to have all of the facts of the situation. This is a matter for judicious alertness.

Chapter 9

CONTINUUM OF CARE

SERVICES TO children and their families may be arranged along a continuum of care, ranging from least socially restrictive to most socially restrictive. The principle under which this continuum is used is directly analagous to the use of the familiar medical continuum of services.

The medical continuum ranges from outpatient treatment through extended care nursing service, then through the general hospital population and intensive care to the operating room.

The patient moves as far into that continuum in the direction of intensity of care as his medical needs require; as soon as possible he moves back up the continuum to less intensive care. For example, the patient with a coronary goes to the intensive care unit, stays there as long as necessary, then moves into the general hospital population and then goes home. He does not need the operating room; he cannot be treated on an outpatient basis.

The person who needs an appendectomy goes directly to the operating room (most intensive care), then moves to the recovery room, then to the general hospital population, and then back home.

The continuum in the human service field (See diagram on following page) ranges from service to the family in its own home (family support system) through foster homes, to group homes, and finally to institutional programs of graduated intensity and restrictiveness.

The operating principle here is exactly the same as in the medical continuum, for each unit of the continuum has discrete strengths and weaknesses, and any one might be appropriate for a specific child or family of a given point in its development.

A CONTINUUM OF SERVICES FOR CHILDREN, YOUTH, AND THEIR FAMILIES

← Least Socially Restrictive — Most Socially Restrictive →

COMMUNITY BASED

- Family Support Systems
- Foster Homes
  - Traditional
  - Specialized
- Group Homes
- Community-Oriented Institution

Residential Care Institutions

- Residential Treatment Non-Hospital
- Residential Treatment Hospital
- Psychiatric Hospital

FAMILY ORIENTED

It should be noted that all services are family-oriented. Additionally, services from the left to just beyond the midpoint of the continuum are community-based; that is, in as many ways as possible, the consumers of these services (children and/or their families) participate in as many normal community activities as is within their capacity.

From just beyond the midpoint to the righthand end of the continuum, all of which are institutional settings, more and more services are offered within the institutional setting, for either consumers of these services are not able to move back and forth between institution and community, the services are not available in the community, or services can be provided more efficiently within the institution. At the extreme right end of the continuum are the most socially restrictive placements, the locked psychiatric ward or the locked facility for delinquents. As soon as residents are able to utilize community resources, they should start back toward less restrictive services.

Historically, children who have been removed from their families have been placed at one point on the continuum as a terminal placement. Children who are placed in foster care tend to be left in foster care, frequently in a succession of foster homes, without really having their needs assessed and without having a determination made of how the strengths of that particular type of placement fit those needs.

Similarly, children have been left for long years in institutional care.

A continuum demands that the system provide fluidity among its parts. One child may require institutional care, group home care, and foster family care in succession; another child may appropriately move from home into foster family care (or into group home care or into institutional care) and then back home.

Too often, children have been moved from one type of care into another type of care only under the emergency of having the child's behavior become totally intolerable in a given situation and, in desperation, the placing worker blindly attempts a different resource, perhaps of the same kind. Thus, we have children entering institutions who have been in as many as sixteen, twenty-five or more different foster family homes, the result of a somewhat heroic, but ill-advised and inappropriate determination by some worker to compel a child to succeed in a type of placement which obviously is unable to meet his needs.

Children who move from placement to placement, irrespective of the type of placement, are subjected to what has been called "total transfer." That is to say, when a child leaves one foster home for another, he is required to sever all relationships with the foster home—he is "totally transferred" to the new placement.

Almost no one but a child in alternate care is required to go through such a fragmentation of life and relationships. The arbitrary and frequently capricious termination of all previous relationships undermines the feeling of worthfulness of a child, and his growing sense of distrust usually has a direct and negative bearing upon his adjustment in the next placement. No one should be compelled to sever one relationship in order to start another.

Placement, that is, moving a child from his own home into alternate care or moving a child from one placement to another, is a process, not an act, and persons who have meaning to the child in one placement setting should be involved in the process of placement in a new facility in order to provide strength, security, and a sense of continuity to the child.

Parents should be involved in the initial placement and in all subsequent re-placements; foster parents from one foster home should accompany the child to his new foster home or to the institution; and any other persons who have had meaning to him should be involved in the process.

The Board's responsibility with respect to a continuum of care is, first, to ensure that professional principles are operative in the agency program. This is basically the function of the Program Committee.

Secondly, the Board must ensure that relationships are maintained with other agencies of the child welfare system and that fluidity among the parts of the system exists. The Board may ask various questions:

> How many children are released according to the case plan, as contrasted to those who are expelled or who leave under other adverse circumstances?
>
> How many children are released to the referring agency as contrasted to those who are moved by plan to other child care facilities or services?
>
> Do case plans indicate long-range plans for the child, e.g., initial use of institutional care to prepare the child to accept foster family care?
>
> In what proportion of cases does the institution staff consider its work with a child to have been successful?

With what other agencies does this institution have working relationships so that children may be transferred with relative ease from one facility to another?

What evidence can the administration provide that fluidity exists among the several parts of the continuum of care?

Chapter 10

PERMANENCY PLANNING

ONE OF THE MOST significant developments in child welfare has been an organized and carefully conceptualized effort to reduce the number of children who have been "lost in the drift" of alternate care. Historically, children have been placed in foster homes or in institutions with the original intention that the placement would be temporary, pending a change of circumstances accidentally or by default.

Frequently the months and years stretch out, and the children remain in alternate care, often drifting from one placement to another, legally tied to their families, but in fact cut off from those families — and increasingly uncertain of where or to whom they really belong and inevitably with the increasing feeling that they not only belong to no one, but also deserve to belong to no one.

To prevent this being "lost in drift," the concept of "permanency planning" was developed. Permanency planning applies to children who for any reason whatever are threatened with separation from their families.

Briefly stated, in permanency planning every effort is made to keep the family intact. If this is impossible, specific steps are taken at the time of separation to ensure that within a reasonable time permanent plans will be made for the child, either to return home or to be placed permanently, by plan, in some form of alternate care.

Permanency planning recognizes the artificial nature of any placement and seeks to guarantee that any temporary placement will be, indeed, temporary.

Permanency planning includes careful assessment at the time of placement of the likelihood that parents or relatives may be able to resume full-time care. Steps are taken to offer help to the family to assist them in regaining or developing that capacity. Individual, marital, or family counseling, conjoint family treatment, parenting-skills training, communications training, employment or vocational assistance, referral to specialized resources, and any and every available source of help is offered to the family in an attempt to keep the family intact and functioning. Only when these attempts have failed and the child remains at risk of permanent damage is the child removed from the home.

When placement is necessary, the family/child situation is monitored carefully during the first eighteen months of placement, and if the parents show little or no progress toward resuming their parental responsibility, permanent plans for the child apart from the family are initiated in order that the child may acquire a stable, permanent foundation for growth and development.

If, after eighteen months in placement, there is no indication as to when the parents will be able resume full-time care, steps are taken to terminate parental rights and to free the child for adoption. The eighteen-month period is used because research has shown that a child who is in placement for more than eighteen months likely will never return home.

Under permanency planning, the preferred sequence of work with children and their families is as follows:

1. Services to the family and child are provided in the family home in an effort to keep the family intact. If these efforts fail, the child will be placed with . . .

2. Relatives. If relatives are unavailable or cannot accept the child, the child will be placed in an . . .

3. Adoptive home. Parental rights will be terminated so that the child can have a new, permanent family. If adoption is not feasible or must be delayed, the child will be placed in a . . .

4. Foster family home. If the child cannot fit into a foster family home or if no foster family home is available, the child will be placed in a . . .

5. Community-based group home. If he cannot be accepted into a group home or if no group home is availabe, he will be placed in an . . .

6. Institution which is no more than 150 miles from his home.

Permanency planning has four characteristics of permanence:

First, "permanent" describes intent. A permanent home is not one that is certain to last forever, but one that is intended to last indefinitely. Permanency planning means clarifying the intent of placement, and, during temporary care, keeping alive a plan for permanence.

Second, permanent means commitment and continuity in the child's relationships. A permanent family will survive geographic moves and the vicissitudes of life, because belonging to a permanent family involves commitment. Whether the child is with his original parents, with adoptive parents, or with long-term foster parents, a permanent family means assuming that all share a common future.

Third, a permanent family is one in which the sense of belonging is rooted in cultural norms and has definitive legal status. In our society, parents are expected to provide nurture for the child and to protect his rights, welfare, and interests. When parental inadequacy or family dysfunction has been sufficient to warrant separation of child and family, termination of parental rights, either voluntary or enforced, is a means of ensuring permanent nurture for the child. Permanency provides continuity for the child.

Finally, permanence means respected social status. Temporary placements can avoid stigma to a degree because they have an acceptable temporary purpose. Prolonged placement, however, either in foster family care or in institutional care, reveals the second-class status of such foster care.

There are variations on this theme, of course. Foster family care is not usually appropriate as an initial placement for an adolescent.

For the middle or late teenager, adoption may be inappropriate, and the goal may be independent living, but with a permanent placement, perhaps in a community-based group home, in the interim.

In other cases, professional considerations indicate the appropriateness of permanent foster family care instead of adoption. When the plan is for permanent foster family care, the agency is well advised to enter into an agreement with the foster family that the child will remain with the foster family until his maturity. A written agreement to this effect gives the foster family greater freedom to plan on its own, and it protects the foster family from a change of plans caused by a change of social workers. The intent of the agency with respect to the child is clear for all to see.

In the institutional setting, the implications of permanency planning are several:

1. To what degree are parents encouraged by the institution—and, where necessary, gently compelled—to remain actively involved in the life of their child(ren)?

2. To what degree are both staff and family aware that each must support the other if the child is to be well served; to what degreee are

parents encouraged to discharge as many parental functions as are within their capabilities, e.g., taking the child clothes shopping, signing report cards, visiting on campus, participating in cottage life, etc. The institution staff will have to take the initiative in most cases, because the parent feels powerless when confronted by an institution.

3. To what degree is the total institutional staff molded into a single team, each member of which is trained in the philosophy and techniques of child care and oriented to being supportive not only of other staff, but of parents of children in care?

4. What help do staff members get in learning to deal with parents of children in care? Visiting parents are not always easy to get along with, especially until they experience a warm reception in the institution. They come to the institution with feelings of various kinds: guilt that their child is not living with them; a sense of inadequacy as parents; apprehension about staff who are providing care for their child; a sense of intimidation at the sight of a large and well-maintained physical facility; and other feelings which find their expression in negative behaviors. Only through interaction with sensitive and caring staff can they overcome these feelings and begin to relax and interact on a dispassionate, one-to-one basis.

5. To what degree do staff members keep parents informed of high points in the child's life when the child is in residence, e.g., sending letters or postcards to announce the child's participation in a school play, his first A, selection for the basketball team; sending the parents pictures of the child periodically, etc., and encouraging the parents to attend whatever activities of the child they can?

6. To what degree are residents prepared for life after the institution?

7. For the older resident, in what ways does he learn how to live independently?

The principles of permanency planning are not an option for the institution. Permanency planning is the official policy of the U.S. Department of Health and Human Services, which has provided leadership in permanency planning. States are mandated to follow.

Additionally, and perhaps more important, permanency planning is one of the best guarantees that children will be well served.

BIBLIOGRAPHY

Didactic Systems, Inc.: THE CITIZEN BOARD IN VOLUNTARY AGENCIES. Volunteer Leadership Development Program, United Way of America, 1979.

Frey, Anne C. and Patricia J. Lindeman (Ed.) EVALUATION CONCEPTS AND AGENCY SELF-EVALUATION METHODS; A HANDBOOK. Volunteer Leadership Development Program, United Way of America, 1981.

Lindeman, Patricia J.: QUICK EVALUATION MODELS FOR ASSESSING ORGANIZATIONAL PERFORMANCE. Volunteer Leadership Development Program, United Way of America, 1979.

Rose, Carol M. SOME EMERGING ISSUES IN LEGAL LIABILITY OF CHILDREN'S AGENCIES. New York, Child Welfare League of America, 1978.

Schoderbek, Peter P.: THE BOARD AND ITS RESPONSIBILITIES. Volunteer Leadership Development Program, United Way of America, 1983.

Schoderbek, Peter P.: PERSONNEL ADMINISTRATION IN THE VOLUNTARY AGENCY. Volunteer Leadership Development Program, United Way of America, 1983.

Schoderbek, Peter P.: VOLUNTEER AND STAFF RESPONSIBILITIES. Volunteer Leadership Development Program, United Way of America, 1979.

Schoderbek, Peter P.: THE EFFECTIVE USE OF COMMITTEES. Volunteer Leadership Development Program, United Way of America, 1979.

Tropman, John E. and Patricia J. Lindeman: THE CRUCIAL RELATIONSHIP; COMMUNITY AGENCIES AND COMMUNITY STRUCTURE. Volunteer Leadership Development Program, United Way of America, 1979.

Valentine, Joseph W.: THE AGENCY AND THE COMMUNITY. Volunteer Leadership Development Program, United Way of America, 1979.

INDEX

A

Adhoc committees, 55
Administrator, use of title, 38
Archives of institution, maintenance of, 72–73

B

Board luncheon, 91–92
Board of Directors
    accountability of funds and property, 10
    administrative structure, 11–12
    and survival of institution, 4
    Board meeting (*see* Board meeting)
    budget (*see* Budget)
    committees (*see* Committees)
    common misuses of, viii
    documents kept by, 11
    importance of, vii
    individual Board member responsibilities, 16–18, 97
    interaction with children in care, 52–53
    long-range planning by, 5–7
    mission statement, 5
    organization of (*see* Board organization)
    policy development by, 10–11
    program of excellence maintained, 13–14
    property of institution, 14–16
    purpose, 5
    relationships with staff of institution (*see* Board/staff relationships)
    responsibilities of, vii, 3–4
    responsibility in continuum of care, 118–119
    review program and community needs, 6–7
    setting goals by, 5, 6–7
    summary of responsibilities, 18–19
    supporting constituency, 4–5
    use of agency assets, 9–10
    activities to insure, 9
    liability insurance needed, 9
    work of, viii
Board of Directors meeting, 85–95
    agenda, 88
    Board luncheon, 91–92
    Board minutes of, 91
    Board retreat, 92–94
    business of, 87–91
    purpose of, 85
    setting, 86–87
    summary, 94–95
    use of annual calendar, 90
Board organization
    By-laws of, 24
    committee assignments, 27–28
    composition of, 21
    consumer representation on, 22
    frequency of meetings, 24, 25
    orientation to, 26
    recruitment of members, 25–26
    reimbursement of members, 28–29
    size of Board, 23
    skills desired for membership on, 21–22
    term of office, 24–25
    use of members, 26–27
    use single Board, 23
    variations used, 23
Board retreat, 92
Board/staff relationships
    Board of Directors (*see* Board of Directors)
    child care workers (*see* Child care workers)
    executive director (*see* Executive director)
    institution staff (*see* Institution staff)
    route of communication, 50
        exceptions, 51
    settling disagreements, 49–50
    summary, 53
    tasks of, 40–43

Board/staff relationships (*continued*)
    use evaluation questionnaire, 51–52
Budget
    development of, 66–67
    endowment, 8, 76–77
    fund-raising, 8–9
    purchase of services fees, 8
    responsibility of Board for, 7
    role Budget Committee (*see* Budget and Finance Committee)
    role executive director, 7
Budget and Finance Committee
    assignment, 56, 57
    budget development by, 66–67
    financial report, 67–68
    investment committee, 6
    membership of, 64–65
    monthly report of, 65
    responsibilities of, 65
    role Board Treasurer, 64
Buildings, Grounds and Equipment Committee
    assignment, 57
    instructions to, 58–59
    responsibilities of, 58, 59
By-laws of Board of Directors, 24

C

Child care workers
    as primary change agent, 39
    demands life-space interview on, 42
    description children upon arrival for care, 40
    life-space interview, 41–43
    special recognition of, 45
    working conditions, 43–44
Committees, 55–83
    adhoc, 55
    assignments, 57–58
    Budget and Finance (*see* Budget and Finance Committee)
    Building, Grounds, Equipment (*see* Building, Grounds, Equipment Committee)
    Development (*see* Development Committee)
    executive (*see* Executive Committee)
    function of, 55–57
    meetings of, 56
    Nominating (*see* Nominating Committee)
    Personnel (*see* Personnel Committee)
    Program (*see* Program Committee)
    responsibility of, 57
    standing, 55
    summary, 83
Community served by agency, definition, 6
Continuum of care, 115–119
    as family-oriented, 117
    Board responsibility, 118–119
    range of, 115, 117
        diagram, 116

D

Development Committee, 75–83
    cooperation with executive director, 75
    corporation funding, 81
    director of, 75
    endowment, 76–77
    fund-raising methods, 82–83
    media use, 82
    newsletter, 80–81
    proposals, 81
    public relations, 78–80 (*see also* Public relations)
    responsibility of, 75
    sponsorship program, 78
    use foundations directory, 81

E

Endowment, 8
    family, 77
    investment, 77
    memorial gifts, 76
Executive Committee, 70–75
    assignment of details for Board, 72–73
    assignment to committee, 55–56
    children's records recommendations, 73
    emergency decisions, 71–72
        examples, 71–72
    implementing a board decision, 73–74
    limitations authority of, 70
    maintenance official archives, 72–73
    primary function of, 70
    United Way representation, 74–75
    use of consultants, 74

Index

Executive director
    as *exofficio* member of Board, 37
    Board meetings with (*see* Board meeting)
    Board safeguard, 38
    dependency on institution, 46
    duty to implement program, 12
    expenditures by, 36
    function of, 31, 35–37
    hiring conditions, 33–35
        evaluation, 34
        initial contract, 33
        salary, 33
    hiring of, 31–33
    knowledge needed, 13
    periodic evaluation of, 34
    qualifications needed for, 31
    relationship with Board, 48–49
    report to Board, 89–90
    reports by, 37–38
    responsibility of, 12–13, 31, 35
    role in raising funds, 7
    title given to, 38
    work with Board of Directors, 35
    work with Development Committee, 75

F

Finance Committee, reports of, 67–68 (*see also* Budget & Finance Committee)
Foundations and Corporations, agency support from, 81–82
Frey, Anne C., 125
Fund-raising
    as public relations, 8–9
    Board responsibility for, 7, 9

I

Institution property
    care of, 15
    responsibility of Board of Directors, 15
Institution staff
    as individuals, 47–48
    child care worker (*see* Child care worker)
    dependency of residents and staff, 45–47
    dependency on institution, 46–47
    life-space interview (*see* Life-space interview)
    relationship with Board, 49–53
    responsibility of, 39
    rights of, 50
    task of, 40–43
Institution finances
    accountability of funds and property, 10
    budget (*see* Budget)
    occupancy rate, 109–114
    per capita cost, 107–109
    responsibility of Board of Directors, 7
    use of agency assets, 9–10
Institutions
Institution
    archives of, 72–73
    Board of Directors of (*see* Board of Directors)
    budget of (*see* Budget)
    child care (*see* Residential child care)
    Executive Director of (*see* Executive Director)
    finances of (*see* Institution finances)
    property, 8
    newsletter of, 80–81
    occupancy rate, 109–114
    per capita cost, 107–109
    program of (*see* Program Committee)
    role of, v–vi
    staff of (*see* Institution staff)

L

Life-space interview
    demands upon child care worker, 42–43
    need for, 41
    philosophy of, 41–42
    role child care worker, 41–42
Lindeman, Patricia J., 125

N

Newsletter of agency, 80–81
Nominating Committee
    assignment, 57
    membership, 68, 69
    orientation new Board members by, 69–70
    sequence of work of, 69

O

Occupancy rate of institution, 109–114

Occupancy rate of institution (*continued*)
    cottage as therapeutic milieu, 109–110
    factors in determining, 109
    factors in filling beds, 113–114
    relationships of children, 110–111
        formula for calculating, 111
    time between one and new admission, 112–113

P

Per capita cost children in institution, 107–109
    computation of, 107
    contrasts family and institutional costs, 108
Permanency planning
    as mandate to States, 124
    characteristics of permanence, 122–123
    description of, 121–122
    development of, 121
    implications of to institutional setting, 123–124
    sequence of work under, 122
Personnel Committee
    assignment, 56, 57
    responsibilities of, 59–60
President, use of title, 38
Program
    committee for (*see* Program Committee)
    incentive system, 62
    level system, 62
    quality of issues, 62–64
Program Committee
    assignment, 56, 57
    contributions to Board, 61
    membership qualifications, 61–62
    program quality issues, 62
    responsibilities of, 60–61
Public relations
    by Board members, 79
    by performing children, 79
        parental consent requirement, 79–80
    by staff members, 78
    correspondence of agency, 80
    methods used, 79
    reports of agency, 80
Purchase of service fees, 8

R

Residential child care
    continuum of care, 115–119 (*see also* Continuum of care)
    factors in filling beds, 113–114
    ideal number in a group, 111–112
    involvement parents in placement children, 118
    placement background children entering, 117–118
    principles and concepts of, 97–98
    relationships children and staff, 110–111
        calculations of, formula, 111
        children's problems with, 111
    supplemental parenting (*see* Supplemental parenting)
    time between one departure and new admission, 112–113
    total transfer defined, 117–118
    use volunteers, 109
Rose, Carol M., 125

S

Schoderbek, Pater P., 125
Sponsorship programs, 78
Standing committees, 55
Superintendent, use of title, 38
Supplemental parenting
    as a teamwork function, 102
    children with totally inadequate parents, 105
    contacts with family by institution, 104
    goal of, 101–102
    meaning of family to child, 100–101
    philosophy of, 101
    principles of, 102–105
    problem handling, 99–100
    role of family, 102–103
    role of social workers, 103–104
    service to family, 104
    summary, 105

T

Therapeutic milieu
    cottage as, 109–110
    definition, 42
Tropman, John E., 125

U

United Way, representation to, 74–75

V

Valentine, Joseph W., 125
Vice-President, use of title, 38